ENGLAND IN
TUDOR TIMES

ENGLAND IN TUDOR TIMES

AN ACCOUNT OF ITS SOCIAL LIFE AND INDUSTRIES

By

L. F. SALZMAN, M.A., F.S.A.

Author of
"English Industries of the Middle Ages,"
"Mediæval Byways," etc., etc.

LONDON
B. T. BATSFORD, Ltd., 94 HIGH HOLBORN

FIRST PUBLISHED IN MDCCCCXXVI

MADE AND PRINTED IN GREAT BRITAIN BY
THE LONDON AND NORWICH PRESS, LIMITED, ST. GILES' WORKS, NORWICH

PREFACE

" Lo | reader, here is a well-meaning book."—Florio's *Montaigne*.

In this little book I have endeavoured to draw, as it were in miniature, a subject for which a far greater canvas, and a greater artist, would be insufficient. As the illuminators of the Middle Ages portrayed a battle within the bounds of an initial letter, setting a bare dozen of little figures to represent the conflicting hosts, but drawing those figures with care and such skill as they possessed, so have I set a few facts, a few quotations, a few comments to stand for the life of a great nation during a critical period of its history ; nor have I spared pains in the composing of my picture, whatever errors the critical may find in the proportions and perspective of the drawing. Within so small a compass any portrayal of the Tudor Age must be a bird's-eye view ; and such a view must vary with the bird who sees it. The hawk and the swallow see with their eyes the same panorama spread below them, but in their brains are very different visions. Others who cast their glance over Tudor England will form other pictures for themselves ; my endeavour has been to show in as lively colours as I can the picture that I see, dwelling less upon the more obvious and familiar aspects of the panorama than upon those not so familiar. So far as I have made my picture clear and real I have achieved my end ; and if I have persuaded some of my readers to go and look at the original for themselves, even though they then see it otherwise, I am content.

The illustrations in this book have for the most part been selected from contemporary manuscripts and engravings in the British Museum, the Victoria and Albert Museum, and the Bodleian Library. The Chalice and Communion Cup in Plate LIII are in the Victoria and Albert Museum, and the Needlework Panels on Plate XL, from the Lady

Lever Art Gallery, Port Sunlight, are reproduced by permission of the Executors of the late Lord Leverhulme. I am indebted to Messrs. Sotheby's for the illustration of "Swimming a Witch" on Plate XIII; to the Oxford University Press for the Tobacco illustration on Fig. 46 from Morris and Wood's "English-Speaking Peoples"; to Messrs. Stanley Martin and Co. for the illustration of the Chained Bible, in Fig. 38, from the Rev. Dr. Hamilton's "Best Book of All"; and to the Society of Antiquaries for "Aping the Men" on Plate XLII; also to the following artists for permission to reproduce their drawings—Mr. F. Chancellor for the drawing of a Tomb on Fig. 4; Mr. Maurice B. Adams for the drawings of Kenyon Peel Hall, the Great Chamber at South Wraxall, and the bedroom at Astley Hall, on Figs. 24, 25 and 27; and the Council of the Architectural Association for the interior of Astbury Church by the late Gerald C. Horsley on Fig. 41. The reconstruction of the Fortune Theatre on Plate XXXI, by Mr. Walter H. Godfrey, is given by his courtesy, and the illustrations of Watton Church, on Plate LII, and of the De La Warre Tomb on Plate VIII are from photographs by Mr. F. H. Crossley of Chester, and Messrs. Frith of Reigate, respectively. The remainder of the photographic illustrations are taken in most cases from the Publishers' collection.

L. F. SALZMAN.

CAMBRIDGE,
April, 1926.

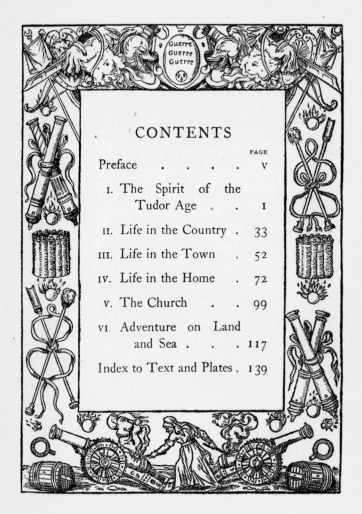

CONTENTS

A DEDICATION

Here, in this BOOK,—a small thing but mine own,—
Something about men's little ways is shewn,
Their art, their books, their dress, their vanity,
In brief, a glimpse of past humanity,—
And something of the fruits and flowers grown.
As SHE tends fruits and flowers with suavity
And mocks men's foibles with gay gravity,
She may find something here to make her own,
Wherefore I dedicate this Book to JOAN.

ENGLAND IN TUDOR TIMES

CHAPTER I

THE SPIRIT OF THE TUDOR AGE

THE century of Tudor rule, from 1485 to 1603, was a period of transition. True that any hundred years in History may be called a period of transition, for History is a record of evolution, but the process during this time is particularly striking. Just so any traveller at the end of a long journey finds himself in changed surroundings, but he who takes the Orient Express passes in a day from Constantinople, with its medieval atmosphere of the East, to Vienna, the mirror of Western modernity. Men in the prime of life when Henry VII ascended the throne had gazed upon Richard Neville, Earl of Warwick and Salisbury, Lord of Morgan and Glamorgan and Warden of the Western Marches, who had played at making and unmaking kings. Their sons saw the noblest heads in England fall, at the bidding of a blacksmith's son, in the dust from which he had been raised to brief authority by a despotic king. Their son's sons saw the haughtiest and most arbitrary of the Tudors driven to apologise to a body of merchants and country gentlemen, representatives of a Middle Class, of whose existence her grandfather had hardly been aware. Looking back on England we see, just before the Tudor dynasty begins, the centre of the stage occupied by Dukes and Earls, with a chorus of retainers ; in the second Act the great lords have disappeared and the Sovereign holds the stage supported by his ministers ; as the play ends the monarch is being reluctantly elbowed off the boards by a grave and bearded gentleman carrying a ledger and money bags and followed by serried ranks of men exactly like himself.

Looked at from another point of view, the nation was growing up. The Middle Ages had much of the character of childhood : a rather charming child-like simplicity of outlook—extremes of joy and misery, a world of clear-cut black and white, or rather black and primary colours, and a reverence for authority, of the Church in religion, of the Aristocracy in politics, of Aristotle or Galen, Pliny or Pythagoras in science ; also a childish inconsequence and thoughtlessness, and a love of glittering toys, such as those belonging to the great game of Chivalry. The eighteenth century had the material outlook of the middle-aged ; a recognition of the importance of money, a preference for solid comfort and a distrust of enthusiasm. Perhaps future historians will view our modern restlessness as that of a man who sees his vigour departing and old age imminent. The Tudor century was the nation's Adolescence. This England of Young Men took life with desperate seriousness and with frivolous flippancy ; it worried over its soul and its neighbours' souls as only young men worry, and occasionally it mocked at God and decency as only young men mock. It was a full-blooded time ; great heroes and great villains, sometimes duplicating the parts, they rollicked across the stage, swaggering and singing ; but the songs they sang were fine songs and their swagger was the sign of self-confident strength, not the bluff of a bully ; and if they showed little meekness of heart they managed to inherit their share of the earth.

At the beginning of our period the nation was in the hobbledehoy stage, busy putting away childish things but not yet ready to think as a man ; moreover, in the last of its childish squabbles, the Wars of the Roses, it had been badly hurt and had also suffered loss of dignity in the eyes of Europe. It therefore required a guardian, and such a guardian it found in Henry VII (Plate II). Cool, calculating and wary, he was the first sovereign of England gifted with foresight, the first to frame a consistent policy, and the only ruler in Europe to accumulate a fortune. Under his personal guidance England cut adrift from old traditions and started on her career as a nation of shop-keepers, a career far more romantic than that of a nation

PLATE II

EDWARD VI AS A CHILD

HENRY VII

PLATE III

ELIZABETH

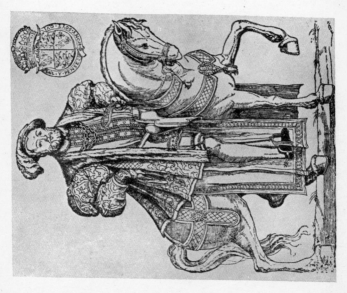

HENRY VIII

of knights errant. His successor, Henry VIII
was the most brilliant and popular of princes ;
handsome, an all-round athlete, a good musician, a l
a passable theologian and something of a physician, c
handed and magnificent, he was for the first half of
reign the ideal of an Englishman and every inch a king
Although as his inches increased his kingliness became rather
that of a King of Beasts than of a King of Men, he managed
to retain the respect and even affection of the nation, whom
he ruled with a despotism disguised under a scrupulous
observance of legality. The ten disastrous years of the
reigns of a sickly boy and a most unhappy queen made the
memory of Henry VIII the brighter in retrospect and
secured the heartier welcome for Elizabeth. In Elizabeth
(Plate III), "pure English" as she boasted herself, the
nation at the zenith of its adolescence found the ideal
mistress in whose service it might live or die. She was
herself, at the time of her accession, young, gay-hearted,
fearless, quick-witted and frivolous and, above all, feminine,
adding to the majesty of a queen the exasperating charms of
a woman. These qualities she preserved to the end of
her long reign, even, with the aid of a red wig and an
indomitable will, retaining a shrivelled semblance of her
youth. By policy or by mere feminine instinct she surrounded herself with an atmosphere of adulation and built
up a legend which gave her in her lifetime almost those
divine honours attained by Roman Emperors only after
death ; so that Lord North wrote to the Bishop of
Ely, "She is oure God in earth ; if ther be perfection in
flesh and blood, undoughtedlye it is in her Majestye."

The light which beats upon the throne may have shone
with a more fiercely critical ray in later centuries, but it
was never more concentrated upon its object than it was
while the throne was occupied by the Tudor dynasty.
During no other period was the nation so identified with
the court. The crown, which for fifty years had been the
puppet of rival factions, now dominated the situation.
Parliament, discredited in the eyes of the people, practically
abdicated its authority in favour of King Henry ; the nobles,
who had played the part of petty princes, became the orna-

ments of the court, contesting for the favour of their sovereign ; the Church, which had withstood the mightiest kings, lost its independence and sank to be a department of the State. The eyes of the nation were fixed upon their rulers ; partly because the eyes, or spies, of those rulers were alert to detect such as glanced askance or wantonly elsewhere. And, in the most literal sense, the spectacle was one to repay attention. As the Emperors of Ancient Rome had recognized that circuses were no less important than bread, so the rulers of the Classical Renaissance owed no small part of their popularity to their pageants and displays. The reign of Henry VIII in Hall's *Chronicle* reads as one long succession of jousts and tourneys, masques and mummeries, banquets and processions, at which the king wore " a cote of greate riches, in braides of golde laied lose on russet velvet and set with traifoyles, full of pearle and stone," " cloth of gold and purple tinsell sattin," or " a coate of purple velvet, somewhat made lyke a frocke, all over embroudered with flatte golde of Damaske with small lace mixed betwene of the same golde . . . with great buttons of diamonds, rubyes and orient perle, his sworde and swordgyrdle adorned with stones and especial emerodes, and his bonnet so ryche of juels that fewe men coulde value them." Elizabeth, less reckless in expenditure, left the provision of such pageants to her loyal subjects but maintained an equal magnificence in her personal adornment and displayed her splendour to her people in frequent royal progresses throughout her realm. Even Henry VII, for all his traditional thriftiness, kept a splendid court, and Mary had her father's fondness for jewels, while her robes were as rich, though not as fantastic, as those of her sister Elizabeth.

The Tudor prince was surrounded with splendour from the day of his birth. His cradle of estate was covered with crimson cloth of gold, with gilt bosses engraved with the royal arms at each corner, and he lay beneath a fringed canopy of crimson damask cloth of gold under a quilt of scarlet, lined with ermine and bordered with blue velvet. When he went to his christening (see Plate IV) it was in the arms of a Duchess and clad in a mantle of rich cloth

PLATE IV

THE CHRISTENING OF PRINCE ARTHUR

THE FUNERAL PROCESSION OF SIR PHILIP SIDNEY

AN ELIZABETHAN DANDY
(*Painted by Nicholas Hillyard*)

SELF-PORTRAIT OF NICHOLAS HILLYARD
(*From the collection of the Duke of Buccleuch*).

of gold and ermine with a long train carried by an Earl, amid the blaze of two hundred torches. If it fortuned him to live to be married or crowned as king he figured as the glittering centre of gorgeous ceremonies, processions and banquets ; but " if I should declare what payn, labour and diligence the taylers, embrouderers, and golde smithes tooke, both to make and devise garments for lordes, ladies, knightes, and esquiers, and also for deckyng, trappyng and adornyng of coursers, jenetes and palffries, it were too long to reherse." Then, when he came to die, his body passed in sombre pomp, in a chariot drawn by horses draped in black velvet, with a greater blaze of torches than had welcomed him to the font, to his last resting place. Magnificent still in death, a waxen image of the king in his royal robes lay on a golden pall above the coffin, surrounded by innumerable flickering candles, banners of arms and sable-clad mourners, while the choir sang *Placebo* and *Dirige* for the soul of the noble prince.

Thus from the cradle to the grave these kings and queens shone resplendent in the eyes of their people, who basked in their reflected glory. Nor did the people grudge the costly magnificence of their rulers. Their splendour was the splendour not merely of Henry or Elizabeth but of England. Moreover, the wearers of these jewelled clothes were men and women ; here was no George IV, no lay figure for the display of waistcoats. Henry VIII may have been a tyrant and a bully and Elizabeth may have winked at a deplorable laxity of morals in her courtiers, but at least their vices were not squalid. It was reserved for the first of the Stuart dynasty to show England a king too drunk to stand. And it is more tolerable for a king to be an adulterer and a murderer than a maudlin drunkard. Whatever their faults, the Tudors maintained their dignity, and maintained it so well that they had no need to fence themselves in and keep their subjects at a distance. No monarchs were more accessible than they. It was far easier for the humblest peasant to have speech with Queen Elizabeth than it is for any ordinary man to obtain access to a minister of a Labour Cabinet. The most magnificent court festivities were open to the public ; so much so, that on one occasion the mob laid hands upon the sacred person of King Henry VIII and stripped off all the gilt ornaments with which his dress was spangled ; the which he treated as a joke. Yet it was this same king who first assumed the title of " Majesty " and made his nobles address him on bended knee. The most punctilious etiquette was exacted from those who might dream of equality with the Crown ; there was no need to maintain it in dealing with the common people. So, also, Henry VIII deemed his dignity too great to achieve lustre from any marriage alliance and therefore chose his wives to suit his fancy from the ranks of his subjects. The secure dignity of the Tudors is the more remarkable when we realize that they had not behind them unbroken centuries of royal descent, like the Emperor Charles V, or in later years, Louis XIV of France. Elizabeth, the last of the line, was the doubtfully legitimate granddaughter of a usurper whose grandfather had been steward to a dowager Queen. It might have been expected that they would display the arrogance of upstarts, of which no more notable example can be found than Cardinal Wolsey ; but their endowment of self-confidence and tact enabled them to show a courtesy which was the constant admiration of foreign ambassadors ; though if, as occasionally happened, any such ambassador attempted to gain his ends by threats, he soon met with such a devastatingly outspoken retort as convinced him that the courtesy was not due to any feeling of weakness.

Such example as the sovereign set the Court inevitably followed ; and by the Court we mean what is now called Society, that class whose doings are chronicled in dull detail in the columns of the more eminently respectable journals. For the Court, at least in Elizabeth's days, was the focus which drew to itself all persons of approved position or unsatisfied ambition. Not only were there the representative of the historic families, the Talbots, Nevilles, and Howards, but all the " new rich," who were as much a feature of the sixteenth as of the twentieth century—the Dudleys, Cecils, Spencers, Cravens and Verneys, neatly fitted out by accommodating heralds with imposing coats of arms and wondrous pedigrees. Snobbery and ostentation were rampant and in no way was it more easy to attract attention than by extravagance in dress. The English, the men even more than the women, were notorious for following every new-fangle of fashion : " Sometimes we follow the fashion of the Frenchmen. Another time we have a trick of the Spaniards. Shortly after, that beginneth to wax naught we must there-fore now have the Italian fashion. Within few days after, we are weary of all the fashions that are used in Christendom ; we will therefore now practice the manner of going among the Turks and Saracens." So that an artist, if he may be dignified with that title, in the time of Henry VIII, por-traying men of all other nations in their right costumes, showed the Englishman standing naked with a piece of cloth and scissors, unable to decide how to cut his garments (Fig. 1).

I. THE
ENGLISHMAN

" Men Proteus-like resemble every shape,
And like Camelions every colour faine.

Bedawbed with gold like Apuleius Asse
Some princk and pranck it : others, more precise,
Full trick and trim tir'd in the looking-glasse,
With strange apparell doe themselves disguise.

Some covet winged sleeves like Mercurie,
Others, round hose much like to Fortune's wheele
(Noting thereby their owne unconstancie),
Some weare short cloakes, some cloakes that reach
their heele."

It was not only at the Field of Cloth of Gold that nobles carried their manors on their backs. Elizabethan dandies wore breeches " as deep as the middle of winter " and so costly that they " would outreach a thousand acres," " triple-quadruple daedalian ruffs," so enormous that they were fit " cartwheels for the Devil's chariot of pride," and were altogether " accoutred in such a strange and prodigal shape that it amounted to above two years' rent in apparel " (see Plate V). Preachers, satirists and playwrights railed and scoffed, sumptuary laws regulating costume were passed ; but sermons, epigrams and laws were in vain, " all falling from better to worse, from pride to pomp, from gay-coloured silk to bright glittering gold."

At the other end of the social scale were hordes of beggars, hungry and half-naked : " for notwithstanding that they be never so impotent, blind, lame, sick, old or aged, yet are they forced to walke the countries from place to place to seeke their releefe at every man's doore, except they will sterve or famish at home. Yea, in such troops doe they flocke, and in such swarmes doe they flow, that you can lightlie go no way but you shall see numbers of them at everie doore, in everie lane and in everie poore cave " (see Plate VI). It is a commonplace of History text-books that this flood of beggary was let loose by the dissolution of the monasteries ; and certainly this was a contributory cause, the local monastery, with its daily distribution of broken meats, acting as a centre of attraction for those who could, or would, not earn a living, and its suppression driving them to seek their sustenance farther abroad. Moreover, one of the drawbacks of the Reformation was that poverty became a crime ; the relief of the poor and hungry ceased to be one of the Seven Acts of Mercy enjoined on all Christians and these unfortunates were harried from pillar to post, from town to parish. Ferocious Acts threatening them with whipping, slavery, mutilation and death failed to diminish their numbers and only made the impotent more unhappy and the " sturdy beggars " more desperate.

This last-named class of sturdy beggars was recruited partly from the ranks of the labourers ruined or displaced by the enclosures of common lands and the conversion of arable into pasture (of which we shall have more to say elsewhere), but still more from the soldiers discharged, without pension or provision of employment, at the end of each of the many brief campaigns of the period. " Doo we not see commonlie in the end of warres more robbing, more begging, more murdering than before, and those to stand in the high waie to ask their almes, whom ye be affraid to saie naie unto honestlie least they take it awaie from you violentlie, and have more cause to suspect their strength than to pitie their need ? . . . . Woorke is undone at home and loiterers linger in streets, lurk in alehouses, range in highwaies, valiant beggars plaie in towns and yet complaine of need, whose staffe if it be once hot in their hand or sluggishness bred in their bosome they will never be allured to labour againe." They formed a regular community, with their own " canting " language and their own social classes, headed by the " Rufflers and Upright men," who robbed not only honest men but also the inferior ranks of rogues—the " Palliardes or Clapperdogen, Abraham men, Counterfeit Crankes, Prygges, Swadders and Patricos " and

2. THE LABOURER AT HOME

their female counterparts, " Mortes, Doxes and Dalls,"—of whose doings those who are not squeamish may read in Thomas Harman's " Caveat for Vagabones."

Tudor England, naturally, did not consist wholly of courtiers and beggars, though they are the high lights and deep shadows which first catch our eyes when looking at the picture. Between the two extremes of ostentatious wealth and flaunting poverty lay the bulk of the population, the great Middle Class, a class difficult to sketch from the number and variety of its constituents. On the one hand the rich merchants and unambitious gentry, displaying a sober dignity alike in dress and deportment (see Plate VII) ; on the other the craftsmen, artisans and farmers, hard-working, respectable and self-respecting. A race whom foreign travellers found pleasant to look upon, " handsome and well-made," and as a whole pleasant to encounter, hospitable and courteous, though suspicious of foreigners and inclined to despise them, their highest praise for any alien being to say that "he might be taken for an Englishman."

Although suspicious and contemptuous of foreigners, the English responded to the intellectual influence of the Renaissance, the re-discovery of the Greek and Latin classics, spreading from Italy. Classicism did not win so rapid or so complete a victory in England as in France, but its effects on art and literature were increasingly obvious throughout the whole of our period. One of the dominating notes of the Renaissance was artificiality. The men of the Gothic Middle Ages lived from moment to moment, improvising means to meet the needs of the occasion. The men of the Classic Renaissance proceeded more methodically, according to premeditated plans. This note is evident in the most domestic of the arts—architecture. The typical medieval house seems almost to be a natural growth of the soil, haphazard and casual ; the typical house of the later Tudor period is obviously designed, regular and symmetrical. It is this symmetry that constitutes the essential difference, and it is this, rather than any loyal devotion to the initial of Queen Elizabeth, that led to so many Elizabethan houses being built in the shape of an E, with a central porch and two identical wings. The older tradition, however, was sufficiently strong to prevent the symmetrical plan becoming as universal as on the Continent and to modify details, as in the retention of the Gothic mullioned windows. In ornament and applied decoration the chief difference between the styles is, again, the luxuriant freedom of the Gothic as opposed to the restriction of the Renaissance with its tendency to geometrical designs. The tomb of Henry VII (Fig. 3), one of the earliest and most magnificent examples of Renaissance decoration in England, when compared with the earlier royal tombs in the Abbey, has the air of being an academic performance, though admittedly a splendid one. Looking at it we are conscious that it is a fine design

finely carried out and are moved to enquire the artist's
name ; looking at the Gothic tombs we are merely conscious
of their exquisite beauty.

It is in certain tombs of the early sixteenth century that
we see most clearly the struggle between the native and the
invading traditions of ornament. A notable instance of
this is the ornate tomb of Lord De la Warre in Boxgrove
Church (Sussex), where the bulk of the decoration is
classical in design but obviously executed by workmen bred

3. TOMB OF HENRY VII

in the old tradition, and shields supported by purely Gothic
angels alternate with others supported by purely classical
putti. In the later tombs, of Elizabethan date, when the
classical style had triumphed completely (see Fig. 4), the
traditional recumbent attitude of the effigy was often
abandoned and the person commemorated was figured
kneeling, upright, or even in the most uncomfortable and
ungainly of attitudes, reclining on one side with his head
supported on one arm. This I am inclined to ascribe to
the fact that whereas the earlier sculptor was conscious of
the tomb as a part of the church wherein it was to stand,
the later monumental mason looked upon it merely as a

piece of design to commemorate a certain person—the more so as the classical design of the tomb was almost invariably incompatible with the church in which it was to be placed. Moreover, one of the features of the Renaissance in England was the divorce between religion and art. Medieval

4. A TOMB IN THE CLASSICAL STYLE

art had been the handmaid of religion. Sculpture and painting had been almost entirely concerned with religious subjects. The Reformation, beginning under Henry VIII with the political breach with Rome which had involved the dissolution of the monasteries and the destruction of incredible quantities of artistic treasures, had declared war on Saints and Madonnas. Statues were destroyed and the painted walls of the churches whitewashed. Of English

PLATE VI

THE BEGGAR

THE NOBLE:—ROBERT DUDLEY, EARL OF LEICESTER
(From the collection of the Duke of Buccleuch.)

PLATE VII

A MIDDLE-CLASS FAMILY

THE FAMILY OF SIR THOMAS MORE

(Both after Holbein)

painting during the first forty years of the Tudor period we know practically nothing ; to be honest, the little we know reconciles us to ignorance. For the remainder of the century it is confined practically to portrait painting. The ostentatious individualism of the period made it almost compulsory for every person of position to be painted. Many of the painters were foreign, notably Holbein, whose sketches have made the features of Henry's court familiar to us (see Plate VII) ; but there were native artists of merit, such as Nicholas Hilliard, the first English miniaturist, whose self-portrait is reproduced on Plate V, and Isaac Oliver, his pupil.

In another branch of pictorial design, the embroideries and tapestries with which the houses of the time were adorned, the change of fashion is also noticeable. At the beginning of the period the subjects depicted are those which had been popular with previous generations ; scenes from Scripture or the legends of the saints or popular romances, and emblematic figures. These grow fewer and in their place we find the legends of ancient Greece and Rome (somewhat imperfectly assimilated by the artists, so that Venus, in an Elizabethan farthingale, is shown lamenting the death of an Adonis in doublet and hose). Scenes from contemporary history also appear, such as the discovery of America, shown in the " nine pieces of hangings having the story of the new found iland," which belonged to Lord Darcy in 1519, or the set of tapestries illustrating the defeat of the Spanish Armada, which once hung in the House of Lords (Plate X). Where the scheme consists of decorative patterns of leaves and flowers the typical change is again noticeable, from the free, flowing lines and fantasy of the earlier period to the conventional, geometric symmetry of the later.

One department of art in which there was not only a change but unquestionably an advance was the illustration of books. The first half of the Tudor century was a period during which Italy, Germany and France produced numbers of woodcuts and metal cuts of great interest and beauty. The contemporary illustrations to English books, where they are original and not either of foreign make or copied

5. THOMAS BERTHELET

from foreign examples, are inferior and crude. From an artistic point of view the blocks used by Caxton, Wynkyn de Worde and Pynson are almost negligible and it is not until the time of Thomas Berthelet, printer to Henry VIII about 1540, that any notable improvement is found. Berthelet's sign with which he distinguished his books —a figure of Lucrece, framed in a classical arch and with a background of typically classical landscape (see Fig. 5)—is a fine piece of work and contrasts strikingly with the sign used some ten years earlier by Richard Faques, in which the Gothic tradition survives untouched (see Fig. 6). Even after this date English book illustrations, with a few exceptions such as Holbein's designs for Cranmer's "Catechism" (1548), are respectable rather

6. RICHARD FAQUES

PLATE VIII

TOMB OF LORD DE LA WARRE IN BOXGROVE CHURCH, SUSSEX

PLATE IX

THE COUNTESS OF BEDFORD
(*Painted by Isaac Oliver*)
(*From the collection of the Duke of Buccleuch*).

than brilliant. Foxe's "Martyrs" (1563) and Holinshed's "Chronicles" (1577) are profusely illustrated,
but the cuts, though interesting, hardly rise beyond
meritorious mediocrity when compared with continental work. On the other hand there are a number
of copper-plate engravings of portraits, maps and title
pages, executed in the last quarter of the sixteenth
century by William Rogers, Thomas Cockson, Augustin
Ryther and others, which reach a very high standard of
merit both in tech-
nical skill and in
beauty of line.

Turning from
the decoration of
books to their con-
tents, from Art to
Literature, our
difficulty is no
longer to find
material worthy of
notice. To attempt
to deal with Tudor
literature in one
section of one
chapter of a small
book might seem

7. A PRINTING OFFICE

to border on the absurd. Yet there are certain lines of
development, certain general tendencies, which may be
indicated without excessive reference to authors of the
period whose works are certainly unknown to the ordinary
reader and, one is sometimes inclined to suspect, to the
ordinary writer of text-books. Once again we start by
noting the prevalent tendency towards regularity and
order ; this time in the very material of literature, words.
The standardisation of spelling, which implies a similar
standardisation of pronunciation, was largely due to, and
mainly achieved by, the progress of printing. Introduced
into England by Caxton in 1474 printing speedily established
its position, rival presses multiplied and books began to pour
forth in a veritable flood (see Fig. 7), compared with the

output in medieval times, though the flood may appear a
feeble trickle in comparison with the deluge of modern
days. Most of the presses being in London, the dialect of
that district naturally established itself as the standard of
printed English. In documents and private correspondence
dialect and personal eccentricities of phonetic spelling continued to hold sway ; so that the worthy steward who kept
the accounts of the Willoughby household could write :
" to Mr. Dygbyse nowrse wen ye kyrstynde his shylde "
(to Mr. Digby's nurse when you christened his child),
" redde clothe to make crowsws for youre sowgearse kotes "
(red cloth to make crosses for your soldiers' coats) and even,
by a masterpiece of perverse ingenuity, convert dog collars
into " dowgke kolerse." But by the middle of the reign
of Henry VIII printed spelling had attained a degree of
uniformity undreamt of in the Middle Ages.

In the realm of Poetry a similar orderliness made itself
felt. More care was spent over keeping the exact rhythm
of the metre ; the rugged scansion, or lack of scansion,
often found in earlier poetry disappeared and even the very
minor poets learned the tricks of their trade efficiently.
Above all, the most classical and artificial form of verse,
the sonnet, was introduced into England. The sonnet
consists of fourteen lines of ten syllables, or five feet, each,
the favourite Elizabethan grouping being three staves of
four lines with alternate rhymes and a final rhymed couplet.
Introduced by Sir Thomas Wyatt and his pupil, the young
Earl of Surrey who perished on the scaffold in 1547, it was
handled with varying success by most of the Elizabethan
poets and brought to its highest perfection by Shakespeare,
who also showed the world what compelling music lay in
Surrey's other discovery of blank verse. The classical form
of blank verse fitted in as happily with the tendencies of the
time as the symmetrical artifice of the sonnet, and its stately
rhythm and sonorous periods made it the chosen medium
for the drama—a branch of literature with which we deal
elsewhere.

Classical artificiality also is one of the notes of the lyric
poetry of the period, with its constant allusions to Venus
and Apollo, its apostrophes to Daphne, Phyllida, Amaryllis

or Astrophel, its too ingenious conceits and its hyperbolic similes, far-fetched and multitudinous. Yet side by side with the artificiality went a love of nature and simple beauty which it is tempting to call medieval, though it is really inherent in poetry, whether of Chaucer or Anacreon. The lyric, especially the love-lyric, is the most characteristic form of verse employed by the galaxy of poets who burst into song at the end of Elizabeth's reign. England at that time has been called " a nest of singing-birds," though one modern writer retorts that it might be called a " cage of parrots " in view of the number of poems which were mere translations or plagiarisms. There was also something of the parrot's scrannel note in a good deal of the singing ; yet hardly any of the singers fail to achieve real beauty, or at least charm, upon occasion. So that an anthology of Tudor verse is a thing of beauty ; but the similarity of all such anthologies is suspicious, and when we turn to the complete works of those poets whose gems are quoted with such regularity we find that there was almost as much poor verse turned out in the sixteenth as in the twentieth century.

One poem stands by itself. Few persons hesitate to admit that Spenser's *Faerie Queene* is one of the master-pieces of English literature ; fewer still attempt to read it ; fewest of all succeed. Though only a fragment of its original design, it is of daunting length, verbose and involved, rising at times to real splendour but for the most part plodding along rhythmically with uninspired dignity. Allegory is one of the hardest forms of composition to handle success-fully, and the allegory in the *Faerie Queene* is even more involved and confused than that of *Piers Plowman*, and, unlike the earlier poem, is not relieved by vivid pictures of actual life. To the student the *Faerie Queene* is interesting as showing how a theme not unlike a typical romance of the Middle Ages was handled by a writer full of the spirit of the Renaissance, and as being built upon two great sentimental interests of the time—the religious struggle with Rome and devotion to the Queen—both aspects of new-born patriotism. But Spenser's just claim to be con-sidered a great poet rests less upon this piece of laborious

C

craftsmanship than on the freedom and grace of his *Epitha-
lamion* and the masterly variety and lightness of touch of
his *Shepherd's Calendar*.

In English prose there are two main lines of development to trace. On the one hand a vigorous colloquialism,
on the other a highly artificial elaboration. The colloquial
style, with its proverbs and folk-speech words, plays a large
part in the religious, and especially the controversial
literature of the time, such as Latimer's Sermons, the
Marprelate tracts or Stubbes's *Anatomie of Abuses*;
and in its more restrained form it is the language of the
Authorized Version. It was also used in books of
travel and adventure and, naturally, in popular works of
humour. The artificial style found its most famous
exponent in John Lyly, from whose *Euphues*, issued in
1579, it derived its title of euphuism (see Plate XI). The
euphuistic writers, aiming at sonority and rhythm, coined
strange "ink-horn terms," delighted in antithesis and
piled up redundant similes. Their sentences were as
overdressed and as self-conscious as the courtiers who
delighted in them. The source of this highly patterned
style was Latin. Latin had been the language of learning
for immemorial centuries, and so remained throughout the
Tudor period, Bacon at the end of the century being as
reluctant to entrust his wisdom to his mother tongue as
Sir Thomas More had been seventy years earlier. Yet
there was a change in the position of Latin after the Middle
Ages : then it had been a language for use, living, evolving
and assimilating foreign elements ; now it became also a
language for study, and fashion dictated that the works of
Cicero should be admired for their phrasing and rhythm
and not merely as aids to vocabulary and sources for quotations. One result of this was the growth of the strangely
persistent tradition that medieval Latin was a barbarous
jargon, fit only for monks and unworthy of study. For
our present purpose a more important result was the importa-
tion into the English language of a great many Latin words
and of something of the dignified roll of Latin sentences.
It is to this that the pomp and majesty of the great Elizabethan prose is due. The writers filled with the classical

spirit of the Renaissance and handling a vocabulary at once wider than that of their predecessors and more pliant than that of their posterity, achieved a splendour of language that made this the supreme period of English prose.

This infiltration of foreign elements, pure Latin and romance, was assisted by the popularity of translations. The Tudor period was the Golden Age of Translation. A large proportion of the books printed by Caxton were translations, though most of these fall just outside our period,

8. "APRILL" FROM SPENCER'S "SHEPHERD'S CALENDAR"

and the year of Elizabeth's death saw the publication of Florio's famous translation of Montaigne's *Essays*. The interval between Caxton and Florio saw a steady flow of translations, ranging from Lord Berners' picturesque rendering of Froissart, most medieval of chroniclers, to Hoby's translation of Castiglione's *Courtier*, representative of the polish and individualism of the Renaissance. Of the ancient classics few were left unattempted. Philemon Holland, "Translator General of the Age," was not content with putting Pliny and Livy into English but "would not even let Suetonius rest Tranquillus"; Sir Thomas North achieved a version of Plutarch's *Lives* which gave Shakespeare, and a host of lesser men, the chance to display classical learning without labour ; and of the poets Virgil found a worthy, but incomplete, translator in the Earl of Surrey and Homer in George Chapman. Most important of all in its effect on English literature was the translation of the Bible. Although the *Authorized Version* was actually compiled in the reign of James I, it is in feeling and origin typically Tudor, retaining much of the wording of the official *Great Bible* of 1538 (see Fig. 9) and of its heretical predecessor, Tyndale's translation (1525–30). Biblical language might almost echo Queen Elizabeth's boast of being "mere English," so free is it from the admixture of words adopted from Latin ; it reaches the highest level of the true vernacular, and it would almost seem as if the breach with Rome which heralded its birth had extended to the exclusion of words of Roman origin.

Closely associated with the English Bible is the English Liturgy, as contained in the two Prayer-books of Edward VI and retained with very slight alteration in that of Elizabeth. The admirably dignified yet simple phrasing of the prayers is largely the work of Archbishop Cranmer, whose Litany first appeared in *The King's Primer,* published in 1545. A certain amount of the wording is due, directly or indirectly, to the writings of Tyndale and other early reformers, but to Cranmer belongs the credit of collecting and composing into one whole these prayers, which constitute a masterpiece of religious expression. It may seem an anti-climax to add to the Bible and the Prayer-book the metrical version of the Psalms by Sternhold and Hopkins, begun under Edward VI and completed under Elizabeth. But, although destitute of literary inspiration, there was an unaffected simplicity about these Psalms which suited them for congregational use and enabled them to retain their hold on popular affection for the best part of ten generations.

The Protestant Reformation, and its literature, in England was closely bound up with the growth of national patriotism. The policy of Henry VII in suppressing factions, concentrating all power in the Crown and causing England to take a prominent place in European politics gave the English an interest in and admiration for their own country, which is the best feature of patriotism, and

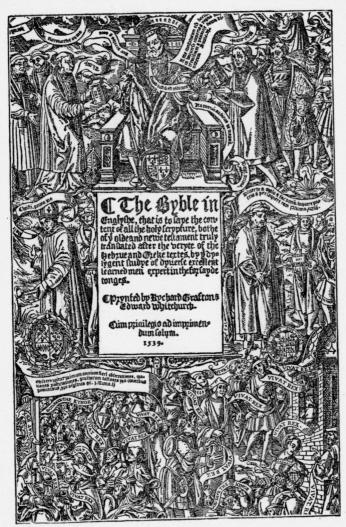

9. TITLE-PAGE OF "THE GREAT BIBLE"

also a dislike of foreigners, which some consider a less pleasing feature of that virtue. The desire to enrich England, and themselves, and still more to humble the Papist Spaniards sent many adventurers on their travels in Elizabeth's reign. There was also, all through our period, a spirit of exploration which was part of the movement of the Renaissance ; men were no longer content to accept what their fathers had told them, either in things of the mind or of the spirit or of the physical world ; they would enquire and see for themselves. This led to the growth of a new literature of Travel and Adventure ; for those who could not go on voyages of discovery were anxious to read the accounts of those who had been. Fortunately many of the explorers possessed the ability to tell a straightforward story in vivid words ; Raleigh, the typical Elizabethan, was not only an adventurer and a courtier but also a poet and a master of English prose ; and many of the scenes recorded in Hakluyt's fascinating collection of *Voyages* (1598–1600) owe their interest almost as much to the manner of their telling as to the matter. One effect of this sea-fever was that when Sir Thomas More wished to write a criticism of conditions in England he conceived the idea of contrasting them with those prevalent in an imaginary island of Utopia, and put the description of its ideal government into the mouth of a sailor returned from a voyage of exploration. More's *Utopia*, written in Latin in 1515 and translated into English in 1551, proved immensely popular, enriched the language with the adjective " utopian " and provided a model for a score of later writers to copy with schemes of social regeneration in imaginary islands of the doubtfully blessed.

Of the other side of patriotism, men's interest in their own country, Tudor literature bears many signs. The compilation of Histories and Chronicles, which had languished in England since the time of the Black Death, suddenly revived. Polydore Vergil, an Italian, was commissioned by Henry VII in 1505 to write a History of England, which he did in Latin ; about the same time Robert Fabyan, sheriff of London, compiled a chronicle in English, and his example was followed by others, notably

PLATE X

ONE OF THE TAPESTRIES OF THE SPANISH ARMADA

PLATE XI

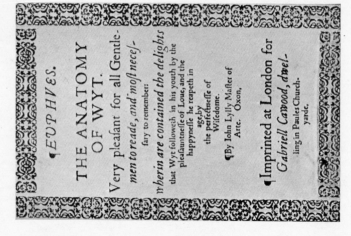

¶EVPHVES.

THE ANATOMY OF WYT.

Very pleasant for all Gentlemen to reade, and most necef-
fary to remember:

wherein are contained the delights
that Wyt followeth in his youth by the
pleasauntnesse of Loue, and the
happynesse he reapeth in
age, by
the perfectnesse of
Wisedome.

¶By Iohn Lylly Maister of
Arte. Oxon.

¶Imprinted at London for
Gabriell Cawood, dwel-
ling in Paules Church-
yarde.

TITLE PAGE OF LYLLY'S "EUPHUES"

A WOODCUT FROM MORE'S UTOPIA

Edward Hall, whose account of the reign of Henry VIII is vivid and picturesque, and Raphael Holinshed. The great interest of Holinshed's *Chronicles* is that they were the sources from which Shakespeare drew the materials for his historical plays, and that the first edition, of 1577, contained William Harrison's *Description of England*, the most admirable and fascinating contemporary account of our country in Tudor days. The second edition of Holinshed, published in 1585, was edited by John Stow, who had himself compiled similar *Annales* in 1580 and in 1598 issued his invaluable *Survey of London*. About the same time Camden produced his *Britannia*, the first systematic survey of the antiquities of England, partly based upon the very unsystematic notes of John Leland, antiquary and librarian to Henry VIII, who between 1533 and 1545 made a great tour throughout England, inspecting monastic libraries and collecting stray scraps of historical information. Further impetus was given to the study of antiquities by Matthew Parker, first Elizabethan Archbishop of Canterbury, who edited and published a number of early historians and founded the first Antiquarian Society in England.

All this mass of literature, of which we have done no more than indicate a few of the main divisions, naturally implies a certain degree of education, not only in the writers but also in the readers. For even in those days publishers did not willingly print editions of works for which there was no demand, and every copy that was bought was bought to be read, the library not having yet developed into a room where comfortable chairs and an aroma of dust and leather facilitate slumber. To attempt an estimate of the proportion of persons who could read and write at any particular period before the nineteenth century is almost hopeless ; the data are confused and contradictory. It is, however, fairly clear that a higher standard of education was prevalent in the sixteenth than in the eighteenth century and that a smaller percentage of the population were illiterate under Elizabeth than under George III. The mere ability to read was probably stimulated in the lower ranks of society less by the Renaissance than by the Reformation, which led to the enthusiastic study of the Bible and works of religious controversy. On the other hand, although England was late in coming under the influence of the Renaissance its effects were remarkable and the pursuit of learning, under the direct encouragement of royalty, became fashionable. The Tudor monarchs both patronized and practised scholarship. Henry VIII could, and did, write theological polemics in Latin (see Fig. 10); Edward VI had more learning than was good for a sickly child of his age; and Elizabeth studied the classics so industriously that she could make speeches fluently in Latin and at least passably in Greek. When the great Dutch scholar Erasmus came over to England in 1499 he wrote : "It is marvellous how general and abundant is the harvest of ancient learning in this country," especially instancing Colet, Dean of St. Paul's, Grocyn, Linacre and Sir Thomas More as pre-eminent for scholarship. It is only fair to admit that there was another side to the picture and that there were probably a good many conservative country gentleman resembling the hunting squire who said to Richard Pace, with an oath, " I would sooner see my son hanged than a bookworm. It is a gentleman's calling to be able to blow the horn, to hunt and hawk. He should leave learning to clodhoppers." It was of such men that Ascham deplored that they took more pains over getting a good groom for their horses than a good tutor for their sons, and that they looked upon the Universities as a last resource for any of their sons who proved too weak and sickly to adopt any other life.

For the Universities the sixteenth century was a time of renewed vigour. At Cambridge the Lady Margaret Beaufort, Countess of Richmond and mother of Henry VII, influenced by Bishop Fisher of Rochester, founded Christ's College (1505) and St. John's (1511). At Oxford, Brasenose was founded in 1509, and in 1516 Corpus Christi was established by Bishop Foxe of Winchester, with especial provision for the study of Greek. About the same time Bishop Fisher had arranged for lectures on Greek to be given at Cambridge by Erasmus, who, however, grumbled at the lowness of his fees, the poor attendance and inattention of the students, and the general lack of appreciation of

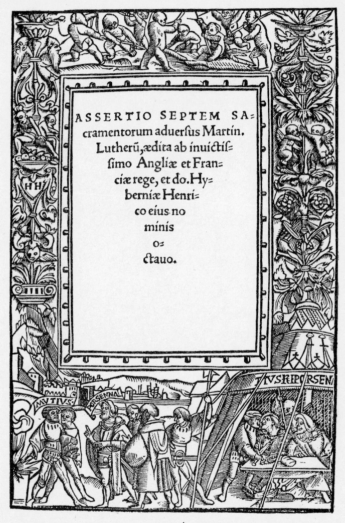

ASSERTIO SEPTEM SA=
cramentorum aduersus Martín.
Lutherū, ædita ab inuictis=
simo Angliæ et Fran=
ciæ rege, et do. Hy=
berniæ Henri=
co eius no
minis
o=
ctauo.

10. TITLE-PAGE OF HENRY VIII'S BOOK AGAINST LUTHER

his merits ; which shows that university lecturers have not altered greatly in the last four centuries. In each university the largest college was founded in this period and in each case received its final shape at the hands of Henry VIII. Cardinal Wolsey in 1524 obtained permission from the Pope to suppress a number of small monasteries and devote their revenues to the support of a new college at Oxford ; " Cardinal College " was still incomplete when Wolsey fell, but King Henry adopted it and, after a temporary suppression, refounded it as Christ Church in 1542 (see Fig. 11). Four years later Henry combined three small existing foundations at Cambridge to form Trinity College (Plate XII). The beginning of the Reformation saw the conversion of a monastic hostel at Cambridge into Magdalene College ; the Catholic reaction of Mary's reign was marked at Oxford by the foundations of Trinity and St. John's ; and the returning swing of the religious pendulum established Jesus College at Oxford and Emmanuel (see Fig. 12) and Sidney-Sussex at Cambridge—all three definitely Protestant, and Emmanuel in particular aggressively Puritan. Inevitably the inrush of the winds of humanism and modernity had ruffled these backwaters of learning ; for a while it looked as if the Universities might founder with the Monasteries ; but by throwing overboard Duns Scotus and all the medieval scholiasts (to whose dry bones no school of whales offered accommodation), they weathered the storm and were able to refit and equip themselves with a new crew of Professors of Divinity and Hebrew, Physics and Mathematics.

The history of the English schools during the Tudor period does not run quite parallel with that of the universities ; nor is it quite as tradition paints it. Popular tradition regards Edward VI as the great founder and benefactor of schools. Actual fact shows that Edward (that is to say, the nobles who governed in his name) was responsible for the destruction or crippling of a large number of schools and that those with which his name is linked existed before his time and were merely refounded by him— with the exception of Christ's Hospital, which was a new foundation and unique in being intended for the children

PLATE XII

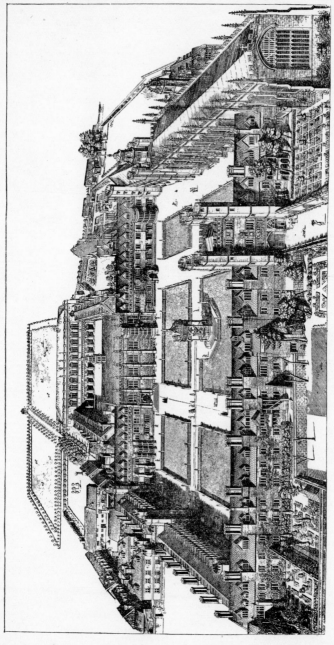

TRINITY COLLEGE, CAMBRIDGE

PLATE XIII

SUPERSTITION :—" SWIMMING " A WITCH

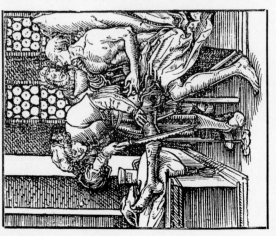

SCIENCE :—AN AMPUTATION

11. CHRISTCHURCH, OXFORD

of the poor.   The proportion of Grammar Schools (corresponding to our secondary schools) to population was
remarkably high during the first half of the sixteenth century.
Some two hundred, including the great Grammar Schools
like Winchester and Eton, are known to us, every important
town possessing one, and many of the schools having from
seventy to a hundred and fifty scholars.   Many others of

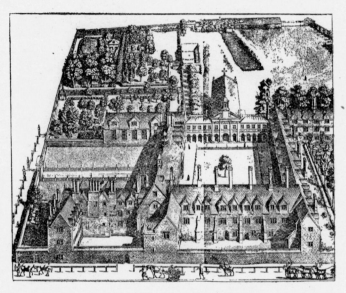

12. EMMANUEL COLLEGE, CAMBRIDGE.

which the records are lost, certainly existed.   They were
not greatly affected by the dissolution of the monasteries,
as the monks rarely had any connection with schools beyond
appointing the masters in certain cases ; but the suppression
of the Chantries in 1549 struck a serious blow at education.
With the Chantries fell the Collegiate Churches, and it
was a feature of the constitution of these Colleges that they
each maintained a Grammar School, as did some of the
Chantries.   The schools were not deliberately destroyed,
but the lands which formed or augmented their endowments were confiscated and a fixed sum of money was

assigned instead to the school ; with the rapid fall in the
value of money which occurred soon afterwards these
fixed endowments in many cases proved totally inadequate
and the school either died or dwindled to insignificance.

Under the first enthusiasm for the New Learning a
considerable number of schools had been founded and in
particular John Colet (see Fig. 13), the learned Dean of
St. Paul's, had re-
organised and endowed
St. Paul's School and
had separated it from
the Cathedral, placing
it under the Mercers'
Company and appoint-
ing a lay headmaster.
As we have just seen,
the Reformation struck
an undesigned blow at
the cause of education,
but against this we have
to set the foundation of
a large number of new
schools during the reign
of Elizabeth, including
Rugby and Harrow.
At these G r a m m a r
Schools the boys were
taught to read, write
and speak Latin ; the

IOANNES COLETVS
Cum cohæ Aomas exculte COLEET E forores
Te doctos inter posthuma fama refert

13. JOHN COLET, DEAN OF ST. PAUL'S

authors chosen for their instruction varied ; in some schools
Ovid and Horace were approved, in others they were regarded
as profane and immoral and were replaced by innocuous
Christians, less eminent for their style than for their piety.
Greek was taught at St. Paul's and a few other schools, and a
little mathematics occasionally figured in the course.   The
pupils were expected to know how to read and write before they
came to the Grammar School, and this implies the existence of
elementary schools.   Some of these were the Song Schools
attached to Collegiate Churches and Monasteries ; others
were kept by clergy, often by chantry priests, who in this

way occupied their spare time and eked out their slender incomes. Here, again, injury must have been done to education in many cases by the fall of the chantries ; but the story of elementary education is obscure. One small point suggestive of a spread of such elementary education during the reign of Elizabeth is that the Middlesex Sessions Rolls show that whereas in the time of Edward VI only nine per cent. of condemned criminals claimed that " benefit of clergy " which was extended to all who could read a verse from the Bible, by the time of James I forty per cent. did so ; but it would be rash to base a theory of diminishing illiteracy on these figures.

The spread of learning did not affect the course of studies in the schools or the methods of instruction so much as might have been expected. That note of modernism found in the universities is lacking in the schools.

The headmasters were usually competent scholars and occasionally men of great learning and even fame, such as the great antiquary Camden, though the salaries were wretchedly small and the general attitude towards the profession was probably that of the Cambridge graduate who said to Erasmus, " Who would be a schoolmaster that could live in any other way ? " For the most part they were compelled by the statutes of their schools to follow a rigid routine in the matter of what they taught, and almost equally restricted as to the manner of teaching by the conservative traditions of their class. Sir Thomas Elyot in the time of Henry VIII and Roger Ascham under Elizabeth vainly put forward schemes of teaching based upon reason and commonsense, deprecated the discouraging effects of savage punishments and urged the claims of kindness and encouragement. For centuries learning had been presented to boys in the driest and most unpalatable form and forced upon their dejected and reluctant minds by frequent floggings. For generations it continued to be so presented and so enforced. That many men who had been brought up in this way did become ripe scholars was due rather to their own innate love of learning than to any merit in the system, of which the best that can be said is that it engendered a contempt for pain, but at the expense of breeding an equal contempt for learning.

One branch of knowledge which remained outside the schools for another two centuries and more was Natural Science. Nor, indeed, did science progress greatly under the Tudors, even in the free and unscholastic atmosphere. The characteristic of medieval science was respect for the written word ; any statement made by an accepted authority must be true. The Renaissance, Janus-like, looked forward to modernity with one face, but at the same time bent its eyes upon the ancient classics and found therein a scientific system very similar to that of the Middle Ages. For the earlier part of the Tudor century, therefore, Tradition still held sway, and it is not until its close that there arose a new spirit of investigation. It

14. MASTER AND PUPILS

was not until the year of Elizabeth's death that William Gilbert published his researches on magnetism and Bacon his *Advancement of Learning*, which he was afterwards to expound and give to the world in Latin, the international language of learning, as the *Novum Organum*. Francis Bacon was the prime exponent in England of experimental science. Revolting against the tyranny of the traditionalists, who sheltered behind the authority of Aristotle, he insisted that the truths of science could only be ascertained by endless experiments and the impartial collocation of causes and effects.

Bacon threw open a window to admit the cold and bracing winds of scepticism, which were eventually to disperse the smoky clouds of superstition—so far as those clouds can ever be dissipated. Side by side with the vigorous intellectuality of the period persisted the childish superstitions of the Middle Ages. Medicine was still mixed up with magic ; Cecil believed firmly in alchemy ; astrologers and crystal-gazers flourished ; and above all witchcraft grew to be an obsession. Until the Reformation comparatively little is heard of witches ; from the middle of the sixteenth century prosecutions and executions for witchcraft become increasingly numerous. Possibly the popular appetite for the supernatural was satisfied in the earlier period by wonder-working relics, miraculous images and holy wells. When King Henry emptied the shrines, burnt the roods and images, and forbade God to work any more miracles, the people turned their attention to the black magic of the Devil and his servants. Modern psychological research suggests that the power of injuring others by a concentration of malevolence may exist ; but for the absurd, extravagant and revolting activities alleged against the witches, and often confessed by them (under torture, terror or an insane desire for notoriety) no explanation can be found but delusion. A few rare spirits stood out against the prevalent superstition, notably Reginald Scott, whose *Discovery of Witchcraft* (1584) exposed the fallacy of the belief—and incidentally collected a mass of legend, folklore and superstition for the enjoyment of modern readers. But such men as Scott were few and their voices were raised ineffectually, the belief in witchcraft had the support of the Church and the Law and worthy magistrates continued to torment and slaughter daft old women to the glory of God and the confusion of the Devil.

CHAPTER II

LIFE IN THE COUNTRY

"Who that redeth in the boke of the moralytes of the chesse, shal therby perceyve that everye man, from the hyest degree to the lowest, is set and ordeyned to have labour and occupation. . . . And in so moche the yomen in the sayde moralytyes and game of the chesse be set before to labour, defende and maynteyne all the other hyer estates, the whiche yomen represent the common people, as husbandes and labourers, therfore I purpose to speake fyrste of husbandrye."

Until the coming of the Age of Machinery England was an agricultural country and her riches grew from the export of such raw material as wool and hides and corn. Her strength lay in her peasant population, the sturdy, independent class of yeomen farmers : "These were they that in times past made all France afraid." For them the Tudor century was a critical and important time, marking the definite break with customs and traditions of immemorial antiquity. Throughout the Middle Ages agriculture in England had been based upon the manor and the open field. In brief, the whole country since the Norman Conquest had been divided up into manors—estates of very varying size but each the sole property of one lord, who possessed certain privileges and rights of jurisdiction over the tenants and their lands. Of each estate the centre was the manor-house, to which were attached the demesne-lands or home-farm. These demesnes were cultivated for the most part by the labour of the "villeins" and cottagers, small-holders who in return for their holdings worked for their lord ; these men were unfree, practically the serfs of their lord, unable to leave the manor without his permission and, in theory, bound to do whatever work he demanded and liable to be ejected from their holdings at his caprice. Actually their tenure was secure and descended from father to son, and the amount and nature of their work was exactly fixed by the custom of the manor, while they themselves were, as regards all men but their own lord, as free in the eyes of the law as any gentleman. The demesnes might lie wholly or partly in a block, surrounded by hedges ; the lands of the villeins, in most parts of England, were scattered in the " common fields." Of these there were usually three, two being sown each year and the third lying fallow to recover its fertility ; each of these great fields was divided into a large number of strips, averaging roughly an acre, and these strips, divided from one another by unploughed " balks," were assigned to the various tenants ; so that a man who held 30 acres, which was about the size of a normal villein tenement, would have 10 acre-strips in each field, and those strips not adjacent but scattered. In this way everyone was assured of his fair share of good and bad land and none could appropriate the best. Besides the arable, or ploughed land, there were in the manor enclosed pastures and hay-meadows and woods ; the remainder of the land, uncultivated and unhedged, formed the waste and commons of the manor, whereon the tenants had the right to turn out a certain number of cattle, sheep and geese to graze and also usually had the right to cut furze and bracken for litter.

Certain changes in the manorial economy had already taken place before our period. The system of forced labour not being entirely satisfactory, the custom had grown up at an early date of allowing tenants to commute all, or part of, their labour services for a money rent. After the Black Death in 1350 the shortage of labour had strengthened the position of the villeins and this process of commutation had gradually become general, until by the second half of the fifteenth century few labour services were rendered. At the same time the feeling against serfdom increased and a large number of the villeins purchased, or were granted, their freedom and became either freeholders or, more often, copyholders (so called because their title deeds consisted in a copy of an entry made on the court-roll of the manor). The new ideas of theoretical liberty which came with the Renaissance assisted this movement, so that, although villeinage was still sufficiently a grievance for its abolition to be demanded by the East Anglian rebels in 1549, it was almost unknown in the time of Elizabeth and the half-a-dozen cases which lingered on into the reign of James I were merely antiquarian survivals. The peasantry of the late Tudor age were, therefore, personally free—a state not reached in France till the end of the eighteenth century.

Further, the cost of labour after the Black Death, coinciding with an increase in the wool trade and the growth of English clothmaking, had led to landowners converting arable into sheep-pasture—a single shepherd being thus employed on land where once a score of men had worked at the cultivation of corn. This movement, which by its displacement of labour soon produced unemployment, brought about a very serious situation at the beginning of the reign of Henry VII. Every year the great landlords enlarged their flocks, until some had five, ten, or twenty thousand sheep. Not content with converting the whole of their demesnes into pasture, they began to enclose the waste and commons, thereby depriving the tenants of their grazing rights, and also managed to evict many of the smallholders, so that villages dwindled and fell into decay, until in some cases nothing was left but the church, which served as a shelter for the sheep. Sir Thomas More indignantly exclaimed that " the shepe, that were wont to be so meke and tame and so smal eaters, be become so greate devowerers and so wylde that they eate up and swallow downe the very men them selffes. They consume, destroye and devoure whole fieldes, houses and cities." A generation later William Stafford wrote, " these enclosures doe undoe us all ; for they make us to pay dearer for our lande that we occupy, and causes that we can have no lande in manner for our money to put to tyllage ; all is taken up for pasture ; in so muche that I have knowne of late a dozen ploughes, within lesse compasse than sixe myles about me, layde down within this seven yeares, and where three score persons or upward had their livings now one man with his cattell hath all." Tudor literature is full of denunciations of these grasping graziers and sheep farmers—" caterpillars of the common weal," "greedy puttocks," and " right brothers of Cain." Acts of Parliament were passed restricting enclosures, limiting the size of flocks and penalising those who allowed houses to decay ; local riots, and even rebellions, such as that led by Robert Kett in 1549, were directed against enclosures. But denunciations, Acts and riots were powerless against the passion for wealth ; and the distribution of the monastic lands, largely among men newly rich and anxious to be quickly richer, aggravated the evil.

There was another type of enclosure which introduced changes of which the effects were more good than bad. In some manors the tenants, by mutual exchange, obtained a number of acre-strips side by side, instead of scattered, and so consolidated their holdings, and, enclosing them with hedges, formed small fields. This had many advantages, as the separating balks could be ploughed up and the land thus more completely utilised, and the more progressive farmers could experiment and grow what crops they chose in what manner they pleased. Moreover, in the open or " champion " country there were constant injuries to the crops due to men riding across them, animals or thieves breaking in, and other causes, which could be avoided by the use of hedges. So that,

> " The countrie enclosed I praise,
> the tother delighteth not me,
> For nothing the wealth it doth raise
> to such as inferior be."

The farmer's year began at Michaelmas. The first thing to be done was to thresh some of the corn which had just been harvested, in order to obtain seed. The threshing was done in the barns with flails—short clubs attached by rope or leather to the end of long staves—and the grain so obtained was cleaned by winnowing, or shaking on a broad, flat, fan-shaped basket in a draught, which blew away the chaff ; when there was no wind an artificial draught seems to have been raised with a goose wing. The ground, either that covered with the stubble of a recent crop or,

PLATE XIV

A VILLAGE SCENE

A FARMHOUSE

PLOUGHING, SOWING AND HARROWING

PLATE XV

THE PEASANT AT WORK AND PLAY

preferably, that which had been lying fallow, was now broken up with the plough. Where the ground was heavy the plough would probably be drawn by oxen; and in such soil wheat would be sown. In light soil a horse-plough might be used (see Plate XIV) and either rye or a mixture of wheat and rye, known as "blend-corn" or "meslin," might be sown. In either case it was well to send girls or boys into the new sown fields, "And let them be armed with sling or with bowe, to skare away pidgen, the rooke and the crowe." Peas could also be put in and there were other jobs to be done, such as setting the bee-hives in order for the winter, collecting beech-nuts and acorns for the pigs, gathering fruit and planting gooseberries, raspberries and strawberries—the last-named being simply the wild variety transplanted, as appears from Tusser's words :—

> " Wife, into thy garden and set me a plot
>   With strawbery rootes, of the best to be got :
> Such growing abroade among thornes in the wood,
>   Wel chosen and picked proove excellent good."

November was an unpleasant month of slaughter ; for the Tudor farmer, having no roots for winter feed and a limited supply of hay, reduced his live stock and killed off all that he could spare, salting the meat for winter use (Plate XVIII). As for December, the best thing about that month was that it contained Christmas, when the house was decked with holly and ivy and there was

> " Good bread and good drinke, a good fier in the hall,
>   brawne, pudding and sowse and good mustard with all.
> Beef, mutton and porke, shred pies of the best,
>   pig, veale, goose and capon, and turkey well drest ;
> Cheese, apples and nuts, joly carols to heare,
>   as then in the countrie is counted good cheare."

With January work on the farm began to increase ; it was the critical season of lambing, and young pigs might also be expected ; oats and beans should be sown during that or the next month and the early " runcival," or marrow-fat, peas might be planted. So the plough and the harrow would be going whenever weather permitted (see Plate XIV), and there were plenty of other jobs to be done in the finishing of pruning, the making and mending of hedges and fences. If frosts held up such operations, the dung could be carted from the mixen on to the fields and there was always a certain amount of threshing, for bread-corn, malt or seed, as required (Plate XVII). In March there was barley to be sown ; but that and April were busy months for the housewife, who had charge of the herb garden and had also to see to the sowing of flax and hemp, while by the end of April she would have her hands full with dairy work making butter and cheese for which the milk of ewes was in those days used as much as that of cows (Plate XVI). Hops, the growing of which had been introduced into England in the reign of Henry VIII, to the great profit of those enterprising farmers who grew them, would also require attention. June saw the busy time of sheep-shearing, when the farmer must " take hede of the sherers for touchynge the shepe with the sheres, and specially for pryckyng with the poynte of the sheres, and that the shepherde be alway redy with his tarboxe to salve them."

July saw the hay harvest (Plate XIX). The fallow land had also to be ploughed over, hemp and flax could be pulled, and those who valued their night's rest were well advised

" While wormwood hath seed, get a handful or twaine,
to save against March to make flea to refraine :
Where chamber is sweeped and wormwood is strowne
no flea for his life dare abide to be knowne."

With August came the corn harvest, which was the culmination of the farmer's year. For that he had, as a rule, to hire extra labour, as it was essential to cut and carry the corn as soon after it was ripe as the weather would permit. Reapers at the end of the sixteenth century received about sixpence a day with their meals, or a shilling without, a little extra being usually paid to the " harvest-lord " who set the pace, and it would seem that a man could reap about half an acre in the day. After the corn had been cut, bound and cocked the poor were allowed to glean the fields, and when it had been successfully carried and stacked the occasion was celebrated with a harvest-supper of goose and home-brewed ale.

The farm-house, on which all this busy life centred,

was usually a timber and plaster building with a thatched roof ; though by the time of Elizabeth the more substantial farmers were building solid, comfortable houses of brick or, where stone was plentiful, of stone, with tiled roofs. The chief living room was the great kitchen, with a large open fireplace at one end, a long table, at which the farmer, his family and his servants all took their meals together, a few benches and chairs and little other furniture, except a " cup-board " or dresser on which the pewter and silver vessels were set out Beside the fire would be the brick oven, unless the household was so large as to require a separate bake-house. A brew-house and dairy usually opened out of the kitchen, and in the farmyard would be the well, as close as possible to the kitchen, the woodstack, barns, stables and sheds for cattle, waggons and so forth. The labourers lived in cottages, of which the better speci- mens were small editions of the farmhouse, while the worst were little more than four walls and a roof, being destitute even of a chimney, so that the fire was built on a stone hearth against an iron fire-back and the smoke found its way out as best it might through the unglazed windows and door, which stood open to allow the pigs and poultry to wander in and out at will. These cottages, each with its patch of garden, were for the most part grouped together, either round the open village green or along the main street (see Fig. 15). It is difficult to say when the custom of building continuous rows of cottages began, but they must have been exceptional in villages even quite at the end of the Tudor period ; a statute passed in the reign of Elizabeth, to the effect that no cottage should be built with less than four acres of land, points to a growing tendency to reduce the size of the cottagers' holdings and proved ineffectual in checking that tendency. Cottages, therefore, were being gradually brought closer together and their occupants reduced more and more to dependence upon their employers.

Whether the village was collected round the green or along the street, access to the houses and communications with other villages was naturally obtained by some kind of road. A few of the main roads, mostly those which had been originally constructed by the Romans and had been kept in some sort of repair by the dumping of gravel on the worn surface, were passably good even in the winter. Most were very heavy going in wet weather, so that wheeled traffic was often bogged, and the side roads were nothing but cart-tracks and in clay land were impassable in winter or only negotiable with teams of oxen. In theory landowners were responsible for maintaining the roads through their properties, but beyond scouring their ditches sufficiently to prevent the roads being actually flooded and throwing down an occasional load of stones and rubbish they did nothing. Most of the traffic was still, as in medieval times, on horseback, ladies riding either side-saddle or on a pillion behind a man (see Plate XX); but carriages of a kind, great lumbering four-wheeled chariots, sometimes drawn by six or more horses, were becoming common towards the end of the period (Plate XX). Even for a century and a half after the death of Elizabeth a cross country journey by carriage in the wet season was an adventure not rashly to be undertaken; the travellers would probably have occasion to call in the assistance of men and oxen from some neighbouring farm to extricate them from a slough, and would be lucky if they were not upset. Many a great house must have been practically isolated, at any rate as far as the ladies were concerned, during a large part of the year.

Fortunately for the country gentry their houses, as we shall see in a later chapter, were no unpleasant prisons and their lives were not devoid of amusement even in the worst weather. Moreover, when the sun shone they could walk in their parks and enjoy their pleasant gardens, for the Tudor age was one in which the cult of the garden came much to the fore. Among the influences of the Renaissance not the least admirable was the increased interest taken in gardening. No great house was regarded as complete without its garden, and the architect of the one was often the designer of the other. As the houses were distinguished by symmetry, so were the gardens neat and formal, the broad gravelled paths carrying on the lines of the building and the flower-beds, with their geometrical

PLATE XVI

SHEPHERDS

THE MILKMAID

PLATE XVII

THRESHING AND WINNOWING

PLATE XVIII

PICKLING THE PORK

BRINGING IN FIREWOOD

PLATE XIX

MAKING A GARDEN

MOWING AND STORING HAY

patterns, suggesting the traceried ornamentation of the architecture (see Fig. 16). Nothing was more typical of the more elaborate Elizabethan gardens than these flower-beds, or "knots," covered with intricate patterns, outlined in box or thrift or some other low, close-growing plant and filled in with flowers—a style which now survives chiefly in the carpet-bedding associated with the parks and parades of some of our provincial towns. Some misguided gardeners anxious to obtain their colour effects with the least

15. A VILLAGE : SOLDIERS PLUNDERING

trouble, instead of flowers used coloured earths ; but of these Bacon justly observed, " they be but toys, you may see as good sights many times in tarts." In earlier Tudor times the gardens, though formal, were less painfully elaborated and the beds were simple rectangles filled with such flowers as deserve to be cherished " for delectation sake unto the eye and the odoriferous savours unto the nose." The variety of flowers grown was remarkable ; William Harrison in 1577 could boast of some three hundred different kinds in his little vicarage garden, and Tusser about the same time names nearly two hundred plants, including herbs and vegetables, as suitable for the ordinary farm garden, forty of them being " for windowes and pots," including "daffadondillies," "holiokes," "pauncies or heartsease," "snapdragons," "sweete Williams" and "wall gilleflowers." Nobles such as Burghley, Salisbury and Zouche experimented eagerly with "outlandish" plants, and among the exotics introduced about this time were the white lilac, laburnum and syringa, yellow jasmine, sunflowers and larkspurs, the passion flower and the Christmas rose. Gardeners also became skilful in "colouring, doubling and enlarging the proportion of our flowers" so that they were able "to do in manner what they list with nature."

Nor did the Tudor garden depend for its attraction entirely upon its flowers. Apart from adventitious aids to beauty, such as statues, fountains, often equipped with childish devices for squirting the onlookers, sundials and so forth, there were shady walks under "pleached," intertwining trees or creeper-covered trellises, turfed seats, raised terraces, arbours and garden houses, perched upon grassy mounts to command a view. Topiary work of yews and privet cut into fantastic shapes of birds and beasts and men, was known as early as the beginning of the sixteenth century; and the same plants, square-clipped, formed hedges to divide the herb-garden from the flower-garden and the orchard. Fruit had always been popular in England and was now eaten in great quantities and grown in surprising variety, the demand for fruit trees being so large that many market gardens were established, the most famous being that made at Tenham in Kent by Richard Harris, gardener to Henry VIII, which is said to have been about 140 acres in extant. Vegetables, on the other hand, had been much neglected but came greatly into favour at this time, so that "artochockes," cucumbers and "pompions" or pumpkins, as well as all our common vegetables, except the potato, which remained unappreciated long after Raleigh brought it to England, were grown, as well as a prodigious variety of herbs and salads, most of which have fallen out of use.

Besides their gardens, orchards and pleasaunces, all the great landowners had their parks; and all the countryside was full of these enclosures where deer and other game were preserved. Many of these parks dated from ancient

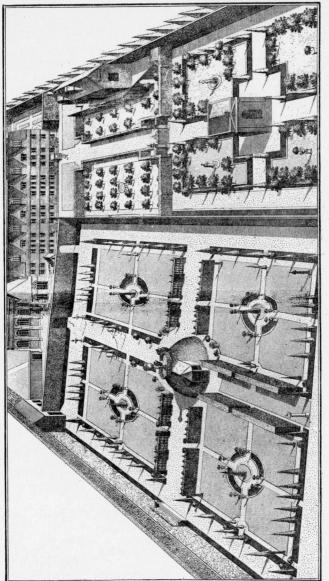

16. A FORMAL GARDEN

times, but many were new encroachments on the peasant lands, made by the ostentation of men recently risen to wealth, " that for vainglorie, worldly pompe, promotion and foolish pleasure will not sticke to pull downe whole townes, subvert whole parishes, and turning foorth all a begging, rather than to faile make them parkes, chases, warrens and I cannot tell what of the same.　And when they have thus done, their bucks, their does, their stags, harts, hinds, conies and the like not only feed within their circuit but eate up and devoure all the poore mens fields, corne, grasse and all.　So that it is hard if any poor mans corne scape their fangs within a dozen myles compasse, which is a pitifull and a lamentable case."　Harrison estimated that a twentieth part of the realm was devoted to the support of deer and rabbits.　" Certes if it be not a curse of the Lord to have our country converted in such sort, from the furniture of mankind into the walks and shrouds of wild beasts, I know not what is any."　For " the decay of the people is the destruction of a kingdom ; neither is any man born to possess the earth alone."　Nor could it be said that the end in view, the chase and slaughter of beasts for pastime and vain pleasure's sake, justified the means.　" Is he a Christian man, or rather a cruel Tartarian, that delighteth in blood ? Is hee a Christian that buieth up the corne of the poore, turning it into bread (as many doo) to feed dogs for his pleasure ?　Is hee a Christian that liveth to the hurt of his neighbour, in treading and breaking down his hedges, in casting open his gates, in trampling of his corne, and otherwise annoying him, as hunters doo ? "

Impossible as it is to accord blood-sports with Christianity, plenty of pious and orthodox persons have at all times managed to pursue such pleasures without disturbing their consciences ; and in the sixteenth century there were very few as averse to cruelty as Philip Stubbes, whose words I have just quoted.　They might admit the economic injury done to farming by careless hunters, but a generation devoted to the baiting of bulls and bears would be deaf and blind to the logic of Stubbes : " It is a common saying amongst all men, love me, love my dog ; so, love God, love his creatures. If any should abuse but the dog of an other mans, wold not

PLATE XX

RIDING PILLION

TRAVELLING BY COACH

PLATE XXI

HAWKING

he who owneth the dog think that the abuse thereof resulteth to himself ? And shall we abuse the creatures of God, yea, take pleasure in abusing them, and yet think that the contumely don to them redoundeth not to him who made them ? " Nowhere in Europe was there such a worship of the hunting of deer (the fox was still despised as vermin) as in England. Andrew Boorde, the witty, wise and much-travelled physician, said : " I have gone rownde aboute Crystendome, and overthwarte Crystendome, and a thousande or two and more myles out of Crystendom, yet there is not so moche pleasure for harte and hynde, bucke and doo, and for roo bucke and doo, as in England." Henry VIII was a devotee of the chase and would tire out eight or ten horses in the course of a single hunt. Elizabeth was a keen sportswoman, and, if she did not display as fierce an energy as her father, retained her ability to hunt longer than he did and still rode to hounds when she was nearly seventy. Like her father she was expert with the bow and on many occasions brought down driven deer, to the admiration of her courtiers. In 1557, the year before her accession we read of her going from Hatfield to Enfield Chase, escorted by twelve ladies, somewhat unsuitably arrayed in white satin, on ambling palfreys and 120 mounted yeomen in green. On arriving at the Chase she was met by fifty archers in scarlet, with gilded bows, each of whom presented her with a silver-headed arrow winged with peacock feathers, and when a buck was taken the princess herself despatched it by cutting its throat. Some twenty years later, during her visit to the Earl of Leicester at Kenilworth, she went hunting several times. On the first occasion the hart took to the water : "There is to behold the swift fleeting of the deer afore, with the stately carriage of his head in his swimming, spread (for the quantity) like the sail of a ship : the hounds harroing after, as they had been a number of skiffs to the spoil of a carvel ; the one no less eager in purchase of his prey than was the other earnest in safeguard of his life ; so as the baying of the hounds in continuans of their cry, the swiftness of the deer, the running of footmen, the galloping of horses, the blasting of horns, the halloing and huing of the huntsmen, with the excellent echoes between whiles from the woods and waters in valleys resounding, moved pastime delectable in so high a degree, as for any person to take pleasure by most senses at once ; in my opinion there can be none other way comparable to this."

Like monarch, like people ; it hardly needed the example of the court to encourage the natural taste for sport. That sport was a necessary part of the training of a gentleman was recognized even by such enthusiasts for learning as Ascham, though they might deny that it was a complete and sufficient education in itself, and it was not unsuitable that one of the first books printed in the Tudor period was the treatise on hunting compiled by Juliana Barnes, wherein the tyro might learn something of the methods and much of the technicalities and language of the chase and of the kindred sport of hawking.

While hunting has continued in favour to the present day, though the popular quarry is now the fox and not the deer, hawking has, to all intents, been disused for more than two centuries past. But under the Tudors it was at the height of its popularity, and grave or gouty gentlemen, like Lord Burghley, for whom the ardours of the chase were too strenuous, could and did enjoy the less exacting pleasures of hawking (see Plate XXI). Unlike hunting, which in the humble form of coursing hares and rabbits could be indulged in by the poorer classes, hawking had always been an aristocratic sport, the possession of a falcon being in itself a badge of gentility. So that humbler persons who wished to capture birds had to be content with the less dramatic methods of fowling—taking them with nets or shooting them, usually with the cross-bow, though towards the end of Elizabeth's reign the shot-gun was coming in and its development during the next century was probably a main cause of the disappearance of hawking as a popular sport. Fowling, though not spectacular, called for skill and patience (see Plate XXII). To approach within range without alarming the birds was no simple matter ; often the fowler would hide behind his horse and so stalk his quarry, or would use an imitation horse or ox to give him cover. Henry VIII had stalking clothes and a stalking-ox, which shows that he sometimes indulged in this form of sport.

For those whose temperament was philosophical rather than energetic there was the placid sport of angling (see Plate XXII), which had its own pleasures without the discomforts of the more active sports. "The hunter must all day run and follow his hounds labouring and sweating full sore ; he bloweth till his lips blister ; and when he wenith it be a hare, full often it is a hedgehog thus he chaseth ; and he cometh home at even, rain-beaten, sore-pricked with thorns and his clothes torn, wet shod. . . . Such griefs and many other to the hunter happeth." Nor is the falconer any better off, he may cry and whistle "till he be sore athirst " if his hawk takes it into its head to perch on a bough and sulk. As for fowling, that is the silliest game of all ; for it is not carried on in the pleasant summer weather but only in the hard, cold winter ; the fowler has a wretched life, "in the morning he walketh in the dew, he goeth also wet-shod and sore a-cold to dinner, and sometimes to bed before he has well supped, for anything that he may get by fowling." The angler at worst may lose a hook, easily and cheaply re-placed, or a fish, but there are plenty more to be caught ; and even if he catch none " he shall have his wholesome walk and merry at his own ease, and also many a sweet air of diverse herbs and flowers that shall make him right hungry and well disposed of his body. He shall hear the melodies melodious of the harmony of birds, . . . which meseemeth better than all the noise of hounds and blasts of horns and other games that falconers and hunters can make. And if the angler take the fish, hardly then is there no man merrier than he is in his spirits." But for all the enthusiasm of Juliana Barnes, whose words, in modern spelling, I have just quoted, fishing was not much regarded.

Of athletic sports in Tudor times by far the most important was archery. The long bow being still, during the earlier half of this period, the chief military weapon of the English, the practice of archery was as essential for the security of the nation as the practice of rifle-shooting in more modern days. Acts were passed in the reign of Henry VIII, as they had been in earlier reigns, commanding every able-bodied man to keep a bow and arrows and exercise himself therewith, and to teach his children the use of the bow from the time they were seven years old. Latimer in one of his sermons says : " In my tyme, my poore father was as diligent to teach me to shoote as to learne any other thynge and so I thynke other menne dyd their children. He taught me how to drawe, how to laye my bodye in my bowe, and not to drawe with strength of armes, as other nacions do, but wyth strength of bodye. I had my bowes bought me according to my age and strength ; as I increased in them, so my bowes were made bigger ; for men shall never shute well excepte they be brought up in it. It is a goodly arte, a holesome kind of exercise, and much commended in phisike."

This last statement is confirmed in detail by an Elizabethan physician : " Shootinge at Garden Buttes to them whome it agreeth and pleaseth, in place of noblest exercyse standeth. . . . This practice, of all other the manlyest, leaveth no part of the body unexercised, the breaste, backe, reynes, wast, and armes, with drawing, the thyghes and legges with running or going." With a six-foot bow and arrows of a yard's length, the Tudor archer was expected to shoot well over two hundred yards, and indeed the marks at which Henry VIII shot with such accuracy in the French King's presence at the Field of Cloth of Gold were 240 paces apart. King Henry was certainly a devotee of the sport and apparently no mean performer, though the sums of money that he lost in shooting matches suggest that he not infrequently met his equal ; they also suggest that he was a good sportsman and that there was therefore no need for opponents to lose tactfully to their royal master. He also encouraged others to shoot and bestowed the jocular title of " Duke of Shoreditch " upon a particular expert native of that hamlet—a title which was retained by the captain of the London archers for fifty years or more. In those days it was the custom for the citizens of London to wander into the fields of Stepney, Finsbury, and other rural districts to practise shooting, and when certain landowners in those districts set up hedges

PLATE XXII

FOWLING AND FISHING

ARCHERY

A TENNIS COURT

GOLF

PLATE XXIII

BOWLS

HOCKEY IN THE STREET

FOOTBALL

which interfered with the archers the authorities compelled them to remove them.

Ball games were also popular, tennis—not to be confused with its modern derivative, lawn tennis—being the most elaborate and aristocratic of the games. Royal palaces, noblemen's houses and colleges were provided with tennis courts (see Plate XXII), and it was even played in Westminster Hall, where during the recent repair of the roof two sixteenth century tennis balls were found, which might perhaps have been skied by Henry VIII himself, for he was fond of the game in his younger days. Less aristocratic folk amused themselves with primitive varieties of hockey and golf (see Plates XXII and XXIII), and there is even a reference to " creckett " being played near Guildford in the time of Edward VI, though unfortunately we have no details to show us what form that national game took in its earliest days. Of football (Plate XXIII) we hear much more—and not to its advantage. Sir Thomas Elyot in 1531 said of it that it " is nothyng but beastely fury and extreme violence, whereof procedeth hurte, and consequently rancour and malice do remayne with them that be wounded." Fifty years later Philip Stubbes wrote :—
" As concerning football playing, I protest unto you it may rather be called a freendly kinde of fight than a play or recreation ; a bloody and murthering practice than a felowly sporte or pastime. For dooth not every one lye in waight for his adversarie, seeking to overthrowe him and to picke him on his nose, though it be uppon hard stones ? in ditch or dale, in valley or hil, or what place soever it be, hee careth not, so he have him down. . . . So that by this meanes, somtimes their necks are broken, somtimes their backs, sometime their legs, sometime their armes. . . . They have sleights to meet one betwixt two, to dashe him against the heart with their elbowes, to hit him under the short ribbes with their griped fists, and with their knees to catch him upon the hip, and to pick him on his neck, with a hundred such murdering devices." That this was no exaggeration is shown by a contemporary entry in the Middlesex Sessions Rolls relating how one player quarrelled with another and threatened to throw him

E

over a hedge, to which the other retorted, " Come thou and do it " and proceeded, with a friend, to charge his adversary so violently that he was killed. Football was then played by opposing mobs of indefinite size, with practically no rules and, perhaps fortunately, no referees. Not infrequently it was played through the streets of a town ; so that it is not surprising that it was forbidden by law and suppressed by the authorities.

Of other country amusements there were many. Swimming (Plate XXIV) was recognised as part of a gentleman's education ; some kind of skating was practised, but whether iron skates had yet been introduced from the Low Countries, or whether the bone skates used in the twelfth century were still the only kind, seems uncertain ; in any case skating seems to have been confined to the lower ranks of society, but Henry VIII and his nobles were not above joining in the other winter sport of snowballing. Feats of strength (Plate XXI), such as putting the weight, throwing the hammer and tossing the bar were popular ; so also was wrestling, in which the Cornishmen were particularly expert. Nor must we omit dancing. The country-dance was a native product and one for which England was justly renowned. More elaborate were the morris-dances (see Plate XXIV), of foreign origin and connected by name, if not historically, with the Moors or Saracens. In these, which were danced by men only, a great feature was the bells fastened to the fantastic costumes, and especially round the legs, of the dancers, which were set jingling by the capers and jerky, kicking steps characteristic of this type of dance. With the Morris dancers often went " Robin Hood " and " Maid Marian " and riders on hobby-horses, and they were particularly to the fore at such country festivities as the May-day games. On the night before May-day the whole population of the village went out into the neighbouring woods to gather boughs and branches of trees, " But the chiefest jewel they bring from thence is their May-pole, which they bring home whit great veneration, as thus. They have twentie or fortie yoke of Oxen, every oxe having a sweet nosegay of flowers placed on the tip of his hornes ; and these oxen

PLATE XXIV

THE MORRIS

SWIMMING

PLATE XXV

A TUDOR STREET :—WORCESTER

SHOPS OF THE TUDOR TYPE :—CHESTER

drawe home this May-pole, which is covered all over with floures and hearbs, bound round about with strings from the top to the bottome, and sometime painted with variable colours, with two or three hundred men, women and children following it with great devotion. And thus being reared up with handkercheefs and flags hovering on the top, they straw the ground round about, binde green boughes about it, set up summer haules, bowers and arbors hard by it ; and then fall they to dance about it." Nor did the nobles disdain to follow the popular fashion, and on May-day of 1510 Henry VIII " beyng yonge and wyllyng not to be idell, rose in the mornynge very early to fetche May or grene bows, hym selfe freche and rychely apparayled, and clothed all his knyghtes, squiers and gentelmen in whyte satyn, and all his Garde and Yomen of the Croune in white sarcenet ; and so went every man with his bowe and arrowes shotyng to the wood, and so repaired again to the courte, every man with a grene boughe in his cappe." All of which makes a very pretty picture of " Merrie England " and a scene of happy, innocent merriment when looked upon from a distance through the softening haze of time ; but it must be admitted that there was a dark side to the picture. Stubbes declares, " I have heard it crediblie reported by men of great gravitie and reputation, that of fortie, threescore or a hundred maides going to the wood over night, there have scarcely the third part of them returned home again undefiled." And if we dismiss Stubbes as a sour and nasty-minded Puritan (which he was not), we have abundant evidence from the prosaic records of Quarter Sessions and the orders of hard-headed Justices of the Peace that these charming festivals, which so attract lovers of the past, were apt to degenerate into orgies of wasteful eating, woeful drinking, rioting and wantonness, and were centres of attraction for idle vagabonds and all lewd fellows of the baser sort. It is not extraordinary that the pendulum swung in the next century to the opposite extreme of mirthless Puritanism.

CHAPTER III

LIFE IN THE TOWN

THE distinction between towns and villages in Tudor times lies both in quantity and quality. A town not only implies a larger settlement than a village but also a difference in nature, for whereas the village is a centre of agriculture, the town is essentially, to a greater or less extent, a centre of trade and industry. Moreover, it may be taken as a general rule that the town has a more elaborate organisation of self-government. The distinction is least definite in the case of certain market-towns, which, being on six days of the week agricultural communities, on the seventh became temporary centres of trade. It is not, however, necessary for our purpose to draw any exact line between the two, as there were plenty of undoubted towns, characterised by the possession of numerous shops (see Plate XXV). The typical shop of the sixteenth century consisted of a single room on the level of the street, on to which it opened by a large unglazed window, the shutter of which let down to form a counter (see Plate XXVI). Some goods would be displayed in the window to catch the eye of possible purchasers, and the shopkeepers' wives and daughters were not above sitting in their doorways to act as additional attractions. In many cases the shops were still, as they had usually been in medieval England, also the work-rooms where the articles sold were made ; but more and more imported goods were being sold in London and the greater towns, and particularly the pretty unnecessary trifles which fashion demanded. An Elizabethan economist writes : " I have heard within these forty yeares, when there were not of these haberdasshers that selles French or Millen cappes, glasses, knives, daggers, swordes, gyrdles and such thinges, not a dosen in all London ; now from the Tower to Westminster alonge, every streete is full of them, and their shoppes glytter and shyne of glasses, as well drynking as lookyng ; yea all manner of vessel of the same stuffe ; paynted cruses, gay daggers, knyves, swordes and gyrdels ; that it is able to make any temperate man to gase on them and to buy somewhat, though it serve to no purpose necessarie."

It was partly to the rage for foreign goods, the ladies in particular despising anything that was not " far-fetcht and dear-bought," that some attributed the decay of industry, whereby " cityes which heretofore were well inhabited and

17. A MARKET STALL

wealthy are now, for lacke of occupiers, fallen to great poverty and desolation. So be the most parte of all the townes of England, London onely except." The crafts-men had also been hit by the steady rise in the prices of the necessaries of life, which compelled the masters to pay higher wages and yet left the workmen worse off. For this rise the greediness of the graziers and their policy of enclosure were blamed but it was also due in the latter half of the century to the enormous influx of gold and silver into Europe from the New World, which lowered the pur-chasing value of the coinage. A further cause of the decay of the towns, lamented throughout the country from Chester to Canterbury, was the growing tendency of the capitalists, and chiefly the clothiers, to move out into the country. Many whose town properties had been burnt or fallen into decay left them to fall into completer ruin to the disfigurement and encumbrance of the streets. For this the unenlightened conservatism of the governing bodies was largely responsible. At a time when trade was being organized on a continually expanding scale and competition at home and abroad was daily growing more keen, the irksome restrictions of local by-laws and gild regulations drove the more enterprising manufacturers to set up their establishments in country districts where they would have a freer hand.

Throughout the later Middle Ages there had been a growing tendency for the government of the towns to pass into the hands of an oligarchy. The Merchant Gilds, originally constituted on a broad, almost democratic, basis, fell into the power of a small group of wealthy burgesses and became, or made way for, close corporations, excluding the bulk of their fellow townsmen from any share in the control of town affairs. Such a development was probably inevitable with the rise of the capitalist system. Nor is there any reason to suppose that these oligarchies were more incompetent, corrupt or short-sighted then many municipal bodies of modern times elected on a democratic franchise. Occasionally a mayor or alderman abused his position to sell his own goods or to favour his friends, but on the whole they were inspired with a genuine desire to benefit their own town and a touching belief in their own dignity and the duty of the poor to be industrious. The attitude of city authorities towards the craftsman or trader was still largely that of the Middle Ages—that he was the servant of the community, entitled to a reasonable profit for his living, but not to make money out of the needs of his neighbours. This was particularly so as regards the victualling trades. At Coventry in 1544 measures were taken against the brewers because many of them, " nothing regarding the displeasure of God, the danger of the laws of the realm, nor the love and charity which they ought to bear to their neighbours in the commonwealth of this city, for their own private lucre," were selling ale at unreasonable prices. Similarly in Chester in 1557, when the bakers refused to sell bread at a price which the corporation considered was "lawfull necessary and suffycyent for the bayker to lyve upon," and thereby showed themselves "rather the occasion of derthe than plentye, agenst the common welthe of this citye, it was thought that they wer no good citizenes nor worthie to enjoy that libertie" and they were therefore disfranchised. Twenty years later when the Chester butchers went on strike, the mayor promptly clapped the lot of them in prison.

The interests of the community were to be regarded before those of the individual ; if craftsmen sent their goods to foreign countries, where they could get higher prices, and so left the citizens unserved, the authorities intervened. Any attempt to corner the market or create a monopoly by buying up produce before it reached the open market was severely punished, and in many ports there was a kind of municipal trading, ships being obliged to offer their cargoes to the mayor, who, if he chose, could take them over as a "common bargain" in which all the freemen of the town could take a share if they chose. Naturally the more ambitious traders objected to such restrictions ; and the more dishonest disapproved of the constant supervision by which the officials endeavoured to restrain their fraudulent activities. Not that the endeavours were very effective, according to Philip Stubbes, all of whose accusations are supported by the independent evidence of legal records. He accused the merchants of making three or four hundred per cent. profit, by holding up supplies until prices rose, by which means "they get the devill and all " ; by exporting food-stuffs and other English goods when there was a shortage in the country ; by using false weights and measures ; by swearing and protesting "by God and by the world, by my faith and troth," that their goods cost much more than the real value. The clothiers and drapers were "cater cosins or cosin germans to mer-chants," making bad cloth, stretching it unfairly and selling it in dark shops where the customers could not examine it properly. Goldsmiths, though more sharply looked after, would try and sell "golde which is naught, or else at least mixt with other drossie rubbage or refuse mettall." Vintners adulterated their wines "so that it is almost impossible to get a cup of pure wine of it selfe at the taverne," and even at that their measures were short. Butchers were as bad ; "though it be never so old meate, toughe and stale, yet will they sweare, protest and take on woonderfully that it is very new, freshe and tender."

Under the control of the corporation were the gilds, who were responsible for maintaining the standard of workmanship in their different crafts. Unlike modern Trade Unions, which are composed of the wage-earning members of the crafts, they had in the Middle Ages included both masters (independent workers, masters of their trade, not necessarily employers of labour) and journeymen, or hired craftsmen, but by the sixteenth century they were becoming more and more employers' federations. The journeymen had been practically squeezed out and the whole control had passed into the hands of the wealthier masters, the entrance fees being often raised to a sum which prevented the poorer members of the craft, who had served their term of apprenticeship, setting up as independent masters. There was also a tendency for the multitude of little gilds, characteristic of medieval towns, to be now united into a limited number of great gilds such as the famous City Companies of London. They still maintained a jealous monopoly of trade and usually opposed the introduction of new methods. Their aims were narrow and selfish and their restrictions on freedom of trade vexatious, leading, as we have said, to many of the greater clothiers and other employers of labour setting up in country districts, to the impoverishment of the towns.

Besides controlling trade, the corporations had to act as sanitary officers and to issue regulations for the policing and general government of their towns. And in so doing they were usually animated by a worthy patriotism and pride of citizenship, which is well seen in the order issued in 1559 for the paving of the streets of Norwich, the preamble to which runs as follows :—

"Whereas tyme out of mynde there hath bene a comely and decent order used within this cittye for the pavyng of the stretes of the same cittye, whiche thing hath not onley bene a great ease and helthefull commodyte to the in-habitauntes of the same but also a goodly bewtefying and an occasyon that dyverse havyng accesse to the same cittye from farre and strange places have moche comended and praysed the same and the Majestrates in the foresight for the mayntenaunce thereof. And for that now of late tyme thorough the gredynes and obstynacy growne into dyverse mens hartes which neyther regards the comodyte of helthe, ther owne eses and ther naybors, nor yet the bewtefying of the cittie, have sufferyd many comely and fayer houses adjoynyng upon the common and high stretes in diverse and sondry places within this cittie to fall in rewin and decaye and some prostrate to the grounde, in the which good householders and cittizens have heretofore dwelte, and also suffer the paving of the strete ageynst the same houses or grounde to decaye and be broken to the great discommodyte and annoyaunce of the neybours and travaylors thorough or by the same and to the disworshipp of such as be Majestrates at this present, in that they do not foresee to maynteyne that thing which heretofore by ther predecessors have ben well maynteyned and looked unto."

Certainly the narrow streets of these Tudor towns, which look so charmingly picturesque to us in retrospect, with their irregular frontages of high-gabled houses (see Plate XXV), must have been unpleasant walking in wet weather and more than unpleasant after dark. Such feeble light as was provided by the lanterns which the innkeepers and wealthier inhabitants were ordered to hang out can hardly have sufficed to enable the walker to avoid the water-logged gutters in the middle of many streets and the piles of rubbish which people would insist upon leaving outside their houses. This last nuisance was modified in most of the larger towns during the sixteenth century by the appointment of scavengers and dust-carts ; these, in Lincoln at any rate, were under the charge of the bell-man, so that dust-cart bell of our own days could claim a long descent.

In addition to regulations for cleansing the streets,

orders had constantly to be made for the protection of the water supply. Where the town was on a river, as was usually the case, the inhabitants had to be restrained from using it for soaking flax, scouring hides and other unpleasant substances, and as a general receptable for rubbish. Wells had also to be preserved from pollution and conduits and cisterns kept in good order. Most of the larger towns had by the middle of the Tudor period a regular water system with public stand-pipes, and in some cases the water was even laid on into houses. London had long had a fair supply of water, but under the Tudors some seven or eight more conduits were set up, from which fresh water was hawked about the streets in wooden vessels broad at the bottom but very narrow at the top (see Plate XXVII); and towards the end of Elizabeth's reign two force-pumps, worked by water wheels, were set up to supply the city with river water. This was particularly valuable in the case of fire, a constant peril. Towns were full of ancient wooden houses, and even the houses built in the sixteenth century were for the most part timber-framed as shown on Plate XXV; chimneys, in spite of local regulations, were too frequently dangerously constructed and left unswept; fire-backs were carelessly neglected, and outbreaks of fire were frequent and devastating (see Fig. 18). " And although men be very ware, yet can they not avoyde theyr neybowres necgligence, especially when the wynde aryseth and bloweth the flakes from howse to howse over all the whole cittie whiche sodenly kyndell and overpasse beyond all expectacion." As measures of precaution leading citizens were bound to keep a number of leather buckets ready for use, brewers and carriers were to put their carts at the disposal of the fire fighters for carrying water, and great iron hooks with ropes attached were kept at different parts of the town for the pulling down of burning buildings. Considering the primitive inefficiency of such methods and the inflammable nature of the tall houses that overhung the narrow streets so that the upper storeys on one side were within a flame's lick of those on the other, it seems less extraordinary that London should have perished in 1666 than that it, or any other Tudor town, should have survived so long. That fires were checked with such comparative success was mainly due to the large gardens and other open spaces that existed in even the most densely populated cities.

Not only was the Tudor townsman exposed to dangers to his health, arising from insanitary conditions which made plague and disease permanent features of town life, and to dangers to his property by fire, but his body and property were alike exposed to the attacks of criminals. Historians talk glibly of the reign of good order which came with the Tudors, in contrast to the lawlessness of the preceding period, but the more one examines the facts in detail the less cause for congratulation can one see. It was a time of violent passions, and if the monarchy was strong enough to suppress civil war, it was not strong enough to prevent private feuds. The country gentry were not above raiding and waylaying their neighbours, and the fields round London, and even the streets of the city, were the constant scenes of duels.

18. A SIXTEENTH-CENTURY
FIRE BRIGADE

Every man carried a weapon, and used it on slight occasion. Harrison says :—" Our nobility wear commonly swords or rapiers with their daggers, as doth every common serving-man also that followeth his lord and master. Some desperate cutters we have in like sort, which carry two daggers or two rapiers in a sheath always about them, wherewith in every drunken fray they are known to work much mischief. . . . I might here speak of the excessive staves which divers that travel by the way do carry upon their shoulders, whereof some are twelve or thirteen foot long, beside the pike of twelve inches ; but, as they are commonly suspected of honest men to be thieves and robbers, or at the leastwise scarce true men which bear them, so by reason of this and the like suspicious weapons the honest traveller is now forced to ride with a case of dags (pistols) at his saddle-bow, or with some pretty short snapper, whereby he may deal with them further off in his own self-defence before he come within the danger of these weapons. Finally, no man travelleth by the way without his sword, or some such weapon, with us, except the minister, who commonly weareth none at all, unless it be a dagger or hanger at his side." The streets of London were unsafe for any one to walk in after dark,

19. ROBBERY WITH VIOLENCE

unaccompanied, and the approaches to towns were the lurking places of robbers (see Fig. 19). Some of these highwaymen were young gentlemen who had impoverished themselves by their extravagance ; others were "serving-men, whose wages cannot suffice so much as to find them breeches " ; and others were discharged soldiers and pro-fessional criminals. As often as not they were in league with the inn-keepers, who would send them word when a traveller worth stripping might be expected.

Robbery, burglary and other crimes of violence and of craft flourished, undeterred by the savage retribution which overtook such of their exponents as were caught. If the people were brutal, the law was ferocious. At the end of the sixteenth century the executions in the area of what is now greater London seem to have been at a rate, in proportion to the then population, equivalent to over two thousand persons yearly in the present population of that district. Yet it was notorious that only a fraction of the crimes committed were brought home to the perpetrators. Death was the penalty not only for the greater crimes but for the simple theft of goods worth more than two shillings, and for a

20. A HANGING

variety of other offences. In the case of treason, an offence particulaly rife, or at least one for which convictions were particularly numerous, in Tudor times, the penalty of hanging (see Fig. 20) was aggravated by drawing and quartering. So that it was a common sight to see a man dragged through the streets of London on a hurdle to the gallows at Tyburn (close to where the Marble Arch now stands), there to be hanged for a while and then taken down, still living, and dismembered. Temple Bar and the gateway on London Bridge (see Plate XXVIII) were permanently crowned with a cluster of traitors' heads exhibited on pikes.

Some idea of the conditions of prison life may be gathered from the complaints of the prisoners in Ludgate against their keeper in 1533. In order to increase his perquisites he discouraged prisoners from having their own beds brought in, as they had a right to do, by putting those who did so in "a vile place called the Lumbardy." Whereas he ought only to charge one penny for the use of a feather bed, with blankets, sheets and coverlets, yet when two or three shared a bed he took a penny from each. From further remarks on the subject it would seem that about thirty or forty prisoners slept in one room. Also he used the women's

21. A MILITARY EXECUTION

ward for washing clothes in, and the women had therefore to pay threepence a night for the use of other chambers. Moreover he would not provide cheap small beer, but compelled them to drink strong ale, which was both dear and nasty, and short measure into the bargain. The prisoners having in this way fallen into his debt he paid himself out of the alms given by the charitable for their relief (Fig. 22) ; and whereas they used to elect one of their number to be in " a hole under the gate " to beg alms of passers by, he had stopped this custom. From all of which it is clear that the lot of those imprisoned for debt or minor offences depended on the good nature of the gaoler and the charity of their friends or the casual public—neither factor being very re-

PLATE XXVI

"THE BEGGARS ARE COMING TO TOWN"

A SHOP

BUTCHERS' STALLS

PLATE XXVII

THE LORD MAYOR OF LONDON

THE LADY MAYORESS

WATER-CARRIERS

liable. A contemporary account of the breaking of Il-
chester gaol shows that criminals were secured for the night
by being fettered and chained together in batches of five or
six. As an alternative they might be set in the stocks
(Plate XXIX). Stocks also stood in the streets or market
place, where they served for the humiliation of drunkards,
brawlers, persons who had spoken disrespectfully of the
mayor, or other such offenders. That other instrument of
discomfort and humiliation, the pillory, was especially used

22. GIVING ALMS TO PRISONERS

for fraudulent tradesmen, slanderers and tricksters in general
—the worst cases suffering the additional pain of having
their ears nailed to the pillory and afterwards cut off.
Women who misused their tongues to the scandal and abuse
of their neighbours were either muzzled with a brank or,
more usually, ducked in the nearest, and not necessarily the
cleanest, pond by means of the " cucking-stool " ; others of
vicious life were shamed by being publicly paraded through
the streets in a cart ; hardened offenders who remained
impenitent would be banished from the city or might even
be " blown out of the town with a bag-pipe."

Whipping, either at the public post, which usually stood
beside the stocks, or at the tail of a cart, proceeding slowly

through the streets, was another common punishment
(Plate XXIX), inflicted impartially on men and women.
It was the favourite method of discouraging idleness among
the poor.   Mention has already been made of the plague of
vagabonds and " bygge beggers that wil not worke to get
their levyng but loge in the feldes and breke hedges and
stele mens frute in somour."   If they were bad in the
country districts, they were worse in towns and worst of all
in London, whither they flocked in such numbers that in
1569 beadles were appointed to watch for them and, as soon
as they entered the city, pack off the able-bodied to Bridewell,
the impotent to St. Bartholomew's and St. Thomas's Hospi-
tals, and the children to Christ's Hospital.   Next year the
inefficient beadles were replaced by " marshals " with bands
of armed attendants, but apparently with little effect. .

The Tudor police system was not very satisfactory and
the Elizabethan constable's life was certainly not a happy
one.   Shakespeare makes Trinculo say to Caliban :—" I am
in case to justle a constable.   Why, thou deboshed fish,
thou, was there ever a man a coward that hath drunk so
much sack as I to-day ? "   Records show us that such a
sentiment was not unusual and that the harrying of the
unfortunate officials was a common amusement.   Nor,
apparently, was there unwarrantable caricature in Dog-
berry's famous charge to the watch, if any man will not
stand when he is bid—" Why then, take no note of him, but
let him go ; and presently call the rest of the watch together,
and thank God you are rid of a knave "—for Harrison
complained that sometimes constables, when summoned to
pursue thieves, would say : " God restore your loss ! I have
other business at this time."   Yet it would be a mistake to
regard them as entirely inefficient ; the Sessions Rolls show
that some of their contemporaries who made that mistake
had reason to regret it.   Probably the two most difficult
problems for the Tudor watch in London were the students
of the Inns of Court and the apprentices.   Students have
always been allowed a certain amount of licence by popular
opinion and the police have always had to exercise discretion
in checking their outbursts of high spirits ; when " mad
Shallow " and his companions from Clements' Inn were

PLATE XXVIII

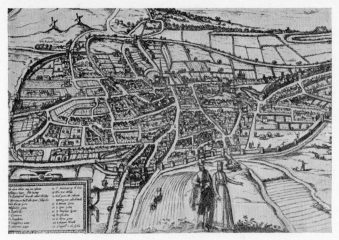

NORWICH

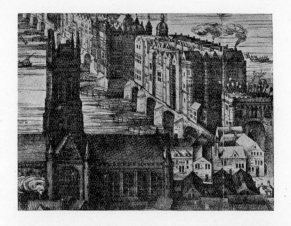

LONDON BRIDGE

PLATE XXIX

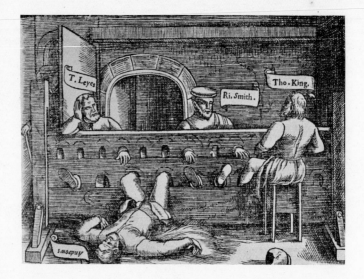

A PRISON

WHIPPING

ranging the town, the watch were well advised to keep out of the way. The apprentices, who might be called artisan students, were another unruly and even more dangerous class. Sturdy young men, prevented by irksome restrictions from giving vent to their animal spirits in games, they were as ready for a row as any Irishman, and a cry of " Clubs ! " would bring a score of them, cudgels in hand, into the street, spoiling for a fight. When they combined, as they did on the " Evil May Day " of 1517 to attack the foreign traders, all the forces that the corporation could muster were ineffectual and the military had to be called out.

Upon occasion the watch, in the greater towns, provided the inhabitants with one of those displays of pageantry so popular at that time, by marching in procession. In London, until motives of economy put an end to the show in 1539, the " marching watch " was held on Midsummer Eve and the eve of St. Peter (28 June), half the constables, who numbered 240, going in the procession each time while the other half kept order. On those nights bonfires were kindled in the streets and cakes and ales set out on tables by the wealthier citizens, " every man's door being shadowed with green birch, long fennel, St. John's wort, orpin, white lilies and such like, garnished upon with garlands of beautiful flowers, had also lamps of glass with oil burning in them all the night ; some hung out branches of iron curiously wrought, containing hundreds of lamps alight at once, which made a goodly show." The procession, which started from St. Paul's and went down West Cheap and Cornhill to Aldgate and so by Fenchurch Street back to Cornhill, was furnished with more than a thousand cressets or torches.

" The marching watch contained in number about two thousand men, part of them being old soldiers of skill, to be captains, lieutenants, serjeants, corporals, etc., wiflers, drummers and fifes, standard and ensign bearers, sword players, trumpeters on horse-back, demilances on great horses, gunners with hand-guns or half-hakes, archers in coats of white fustian, signed on the breast and back with the arms of the city, their bows bent in their hands, with sheaves of arrows by their sides, pikemen in bright corslets, bur-

F

ganets, etc., halberds, the like bill-men in almaine rivets and aprons of mail in great number ; there were also divers pageants, morris dancers, constables—the one half, which was one hundred and twenty, on St. John's eve, the other half on St. Peter's eve—in bright harness, some overgilt, and every one a jornet (or cloak) of scarlet thereupon and a chain of gold, his henchman following him, his minstrels before him and his cresset light passing by him ; the waits of the city, the mayor's officers for his guard before him, all in a livery of worsted or party-coloured jackets, the mayor himself well mounted on horseback, the swordbearer before him in fair armour well mounted also, the mayor's footmen and the like torch-bearers about him, henchmen twain upon great stirring horses following him. The sheriffs' watches came one after the other in like order, but not so large in number as the mayor's : for where the mayor had beside his giant three pageants, each of the sheriffs had besides their giants but two pageants, each their morris dance and one henchman, their officers in jackets of worsted or say, party-coloured, differing from the mayor's and each from other, but having harnessed men a great many."

A contemporary account of the marching watch of 1521 describes the mayor and sheriffs as clad in armour with crimson surcoats, and their helmets carried by mounted pages. It also mentions a very tall canvas giant and various pageants, one of Pluto (or more probably Satan), " naked with a drawn sword so contrived that when he brandished it the serpent (on which he sat) vomited stinking sulphur fire-balls " ; another, by way of contrast, was " a stage on which was a very beautiful little girl under a canopy of brocade, representing the Virgin Mary, with four boys in white surplices chanting." There was also a stage with St. George and the Dragon, and another with Herod at table and the daughter of Herodias dancing, or rather doing acrobatic feats, before him.

Similar movable stages, or pageant-carts, were used by the craft gilds for their performances of miracle plays at Whitsun or on the feast of Corpus Christi. It had become the custom for each gild, or group of gilds, to present a play dealing with some biblical or legendary story. When the gilds were numerous an entire cycle of sacred history, from the Creation of the World to the Last Judgment might be presented. As soon as a play had been finished the cart moved on to another site to repeat the performance, making way for the next play. These pageant-carts were of two storeys, the upper forming the stage and the lower, hung round with drapery, serving as a dressing room for the actors. The costumes were fairly elaborate, including wigs and masks, scenery was naturally scanty but numerous " properties " were employed, especially a monstrous dragon's head, to represent the jaws of Hell, which sent forth smoke and flames most realistically. While many of the plays were clumsy productions, not a few showed real life and dramatic characterisation, and some contained passages of dignity, pathos and poetry. Nor was there any lack of humour and comic relief. The humour was usually crude and boisterous, the humour of the nursery rather than of the drawing-room, and it is not surprising that as the people grew more self-conscious it was regarded as out of place in dealing with sacred subjects. After the Reformation, therefore, the pageant plays, so far as they survived at all, tended to become more didactic and artificial. Meanwhile the custom was growing of performing masques and interludes at Court, and therefore in the houses of the great nobles who modelled themselves on the Court. The masques were ballets in which music and dancing, with the aid of elaborate costumes, told a story or suggested a sentiment. The interludes were short plays, in prose or verse, usually didactic or allegorical. While Henry VIII and his courtiers often took part in masques, the plays were mostly performed by " the children " or choristers of the Chapel Royal and St. Paul's. Topical events were occasionally brought into these plays ; during his controversy with Luther, Henry VIII caused that heretical character to be introduced and burlesqued in such a play, and two plays, one dealing topically with Ireland— and therefore presumably a tragedy—were included in the last series of entertainments at the court of Edward VI : " a mask of Greek Woorthyes, a maske of Medyosses being half deathe (i.e. a skeleton) half man, a maske of Bagpypes, a maske of Cattes, a maske of Tumblers goinge upon theyre handes with theyre feet upward, with two maskes of torche-bearers to them of the playe of the state of Ireland sett owte by William Baldwin and another playe of children made by Mr. Haywood."

Even in the fifteenth century there had been bands of itinerant players who visited the various towns and gave performances of miracle plays and "moralities," very similar to the interludes. During the reign of Henry VIII many nobles extended their patronage to companies of these strolling players, who, when not required for the amusement of their patrons, went on tour, protected by such patronage from the penalties otherwise attaching to their vagabondage. No regular theatres yet existed and the performances were given in the open yards of the inns (see Plate XXXI). A rough stage, of boards supported on the heads of barrels, was put up at one end of the yard ; the rooms of the inn served for dressing in ; the yard itself gave standing room for the bulk of the audience, while the galleries running round it accommodated the more aristocratic. For their reward the players depended on the generosity of the spectators, and they were not above holding up the action of their play at an exciting moment in order to take up the collection.

By 1574 acting was well established as a profession and in London some half-a-dozen inns had found it worth while practically to convert their yards into places of entertainment, the audience were profitable customers for refreshments, and the more unscrupulous landlords could make other less legitimate profits out of their private rooms. Puritans denounced playhouses and those who attended them in such exaggerated terms of abuse that Hell itself seemed in comparison respectable. The city authorities denounced "such as frequented the said plays, being the ordinary place of meeting for all vagrant persons and masterless men that hang about the city, theeves, horse-stealers, whoremongers, cozeners, cony-catching persons, practicers of treason and such other like." On the other hand the nobles, and the Queen herself, openly supported the players, and the gentry as a whole probably agreed with the opinion expressed in later years by that sensible

PLATE XXX

CORONATION PROCESSION OF EDWARD VI

PLATE XXXI

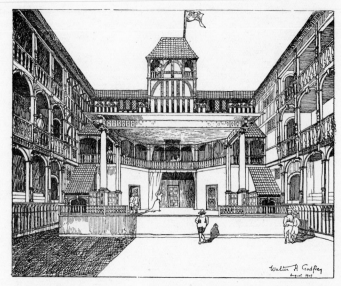

THE FORTUNE THEATRE :—A RECONSTRUCTION BY WALTER H. GODFREY

COURTYARD OF THE NEW INN, GLOUCESTER

courtier, Sir John Harington : " I thinke in stage-playes may bee much good, in well-penned comedies, and specially tragedies ; and I remember in Cambridge, howsoever the presyser sort have banisht them, the wyser sort did, and still doe, mayntayn them." A compromise was reached in 1574 by an ordinance that no plays containing unchaste, seditious or unfit matter should be acted in London, and that all plays must be read and licensed by the Lord Mayor and Court of Aldermen before being performed in public. Also, only such inns as were licensed for the purpose might be used, and no performances were to take place during the time of divine service or when epidemics made such assemblies dangerous. Two years later James Burbage, the chief actor in the Earl of Leicester's company, with the financial support of John Brayne, built the first regular theatre, in Holywell on the borders of Finsbury Field, a spot easily accessible but just outside the control of the obnoxious City authorities. The Theatre, as it was called, was probably round, with three or four covered galleries, one above the other ; the central space, open to the sky, formed a pit or yard, into which projected the stage, with a dressing-room behind and a balcony above it (see Plate XXXI). The whole seems to have been lavishly decorated and painted, and the pit and galleries between them probably held something not far short of a thousand persons. Next year another play-house, the Curtain, so called from the name of the estate on which it was built, was erected close to the Theatre, and ten years later, in 1587, the Rose in Southwark, on the south side of the river, was built by Philip Hensloe. This was followed by the Swan, near the south end of the present Blackfriars Bridge, in 1595, and the famous Globe, so closely associated with Shakespeare, near the Rose in 1599.

Meanwhile the plays themselves had developed even more than the manner of their presentation. It is not without significance that whereas the court festivities of Edward VI had consisted of five masques and two plays, those at Richmond Palace during the Christmas of 1578 included only two masques, one of Amazons and one of Knights, and six plays : " A Morrall of the marryage of Mynde and Measure ; A playe of the Three Systers of Mantua ; An history of the creweltie of a Stepmother ; a Pastorell or historie of a Greeke Maide ; and The historie of the Rape of the second Helene." Of these the first was performed by " the children of Pawles " and " the children of the Chappell " also gave a play, but the others were by three of the leading public companies, those of the Lord Chamberlain, the Earl of Warwick and the Earl of Leicester. Miracle plays and moralities might still hold their own to some extent in the provinces, but in London they had made way for historical plays and the drama of character. Nor was there any lack of writers ; within five years of Elizabeth's accession Richard Edwards had produced *Damon and Pythias*, adhering to the old tradition of rhymed verse, Thomas Sackville *Gorboduc*, the first tragedy in blank verse, and Nicholas Udall, the flogging headmaster of Eton, *Ralph Roister-Doister*, the earliest surviving comedy of the new style. A multitude of their contemporaries have vanished, with their works, into oblivion, but twenty years later, during the decade of the Armada, English drama suddenly leaps into life. Kyd, Peele and Greene, it is true, are, and are likely to remain, mere names to the general reader ; yet they were tall fellows in their day, and Christopher Marlowe, with *Edward II, Tamburlaine, The Jew of Malta* and *The Tragedy of Dr. Faustas* to his credit, was a very giant. The year 1564 in which Marlowe was born saw also the birth of William Shakespeare. Son of a respectable townsman of Stratford, Shakespeare was educated at the local grammar school and about 1586 came up to London and became an actor. That he was ever very proficient in that art there is no evidence, but he was a very useful member of the company, as he soon proved to have a genius for adapting old plays and infusing life and poetry into their dry bones. For such work he was fitted by temperament and circumstances ; he was by nature a poet, handling the formal sonnet and the tuneful lyric with equal and incomparable skill ; he was an actor and had therefore a grasp of the technique of the stage ; he was a man of the people, and it is emphatically in humanity that he transcends all other dramatists. Working at high pressure—he seems to have turned out ten plays between 1591 and 1594 and nine more before 1600—he occasionally failed to "join his flats," retaining from his sources scenes or characters that clashed with his own development of the plays ; he frequently padded out his play with lamentably poor stuff ; and he was not above playing to the gallery with windy rhetoric or cheap and nasty humour. Later critics, overawed by the majesty of his work as a whole, have attempted to shift the responsibility for all the weak passages on to the shoulders of his collaborators, real or supposititious. Others, stupefied by his splendour and possessed by a touching belief in the intelligence of our old aristocracy, have refused to admit that such plays could be written by any one below the rank of a lord—some unconscious humourists even fathering them upon Francis Bacon, a man as devoid of humour as he was of poetry. His own contemporaries admitted and admired his genius, but neither regarded the plays as faultless nor as miraculously beyond the capacity of the man.

Shakespeare remains the greatest of the Elizabethan writers, though *Macbeth, Othello, King Lear, Anthony and Cleopatra* and *The Tempest* belong to the reign of James I. He is Tudor in the spirit of adventure and curiosity that breathes through his work. And yet he is not Tudor, for he is " not of an age, but for all time."

CHAPTER IV

LIFE IN THE HOME

THE transitional note of the Tudor period is particularly clear in domestic architecture. Comparing the country houses built in the reign of Henry VII with those built in Elizabeth's reign we are conscious of a definite change from the medieval to the modern. Externally, as we have already noticed, that change was notably a change from the haphazard arrangement of the medieval master-builder to the symmetrical design of the Renaissance architect. In details it involved the gradual displacement of Gothic features by classical ; the disappearance of pointed windows, cusped tracery and naturalistic carving, and the introduction of columns, pilasters, pediments and conventional patterns. Naturally there was a period of overlapping, when the design was often incompletely symmetrical and the decorative features belonged to both styles, so that at Layer Marney (Essex), built about 1520, we find windows of typically Gothic tracery covered with arabesques equally typical of the Renaissance (Plate XXXIII) and in the contemporary house at Sutton (Surrey) Italian *amorini* are introduced in a façade of which the predominant features are in the old English tradition. Internally the great change is the degradation of the Hall. Throughout the Middle Ages and well into the sixteenth century the Hall was the centre, literally and metaphorically, of every house of any importance ; it extended to the full height of the house, the timbers of its roof being often elaborately worked ; at one end was the raised dais of the high table, often flanked by a great bow window, and beyond the dais a door leading into the private apartments ; at the other end the screens, usually of carved and panelled woodwork, with two doors into a passage, across which lay the kitchen and servants' quarters (see Plate XXXIV). Here in earlier days the whole house-

PLATE XXXII

WILLIAM SHAKESPEARE

THE ACTOR, CIRCA 1500

FRANCIS BACON

PLATE XXXIII

SUTTON PLACE

LAYER MARNEY

PLATE XXXIV

GREAT HALL OF THE MIDDLE TEMPLE

PLATE XXXV

STAIRCASE AT LYMORE, MONTGOMERY

hold had dined and talked and disported themselves and not infrequently slept ; but already by the beginning of the Tudor century private dining and withdrawing-rooms had become the fashion, the family no longer dined in company with the servants and humbler guests except on festival occasions. Such great Halls continued to be built until the seventeenth century in the largest houses, where prodigal hospitality was maintained, but in the ordinary house the hall had lost its pride of place ; the demands of symmetry shifted the entrance porch from the screen-passage to open directly into the middle of the hall, which thus assumed its modern function of a vestibule. Concurrently the old type of narrow, winding stone stairs gave place to the broad wooden staircases which form one of the most prominent features of the typical Elizabethan hall, such as that at Lymore, Montgomery, shown on Plate XXXV. The upper floor, to which these fine, even magnificent, staircases led, now began to assume a greater importance ; no longer devoted entirely to bed-chambers, it not infrequently contained a long gallery, where in wet weather the ladies of the house could take gentle exercise, and where the portraits of the owner, his family, ancestors and noble relatives could be displayed (see Plate XXXVI).

It was a period of riotous activity in building, and has left its mark, a very pleasant mark, over the whole face of the country. Old houses were altered, and new sprang up, so solid and so comfortable that a prodigious number have survived the passage of time and the changes of fashion, though some of the most magnificent have disappeared or dwindled, their very size and splendour involving them and their builders in joint ruin. The growth of trade, the distribution of monastic lands, the flow of riches from the New World led to the rise of an aristocracy of wealth, whose members rivalled the Italian ostentation of their rulers. The princes built palaces, such as Richmond, Nonsuch (Plate XXXVI), Greenwich and Hatfield. Their subjects followed suit, Cardinal Wolsey's creations at Hampton Court and Whitehall—both seized and completed by Henry VIII, " the only Phoenix of his time for fine and curious masonry "— excelling only as he himself excelled in arrogance and wealth ;

so that an Elizabethan writer, whose sentiments are echoed by many contemporaries, complained : " Outrageous is the great and sumptuous building of our time ; it consumeth all the great timber of the realm, which should serve to make us ships for our walls and defence, and within a while it will force us either to build our vessels in strange countries or else to yield ourselves for a prey to our enemies. Also it beggareth the greatest number of them that take pleasure therein and maketh them unable to serve their country ; and there be many more great houses already than there be men of living able to uphold." These private palaces—as for instance Cowdray, of early Tudor date (Plate XXXVII), and Audley End, begun in the last year of Elizabeth—were built round quadrangular courts, resembling in plan, and even in detail, contemporary colleges at Oxford and Cambridge. Such a plan, however, was used only for the most enormous buildings at the end of the Tudor period, though it had been the normal arrangement for a great house a couple of generations earlier, when Dr. Andrew Boorde wrote.

Dr. Boorde, who in 1542 published a manual of hygiene containing more sound commonsense than many similar works of recent date, gave much good advice to such as might contemplate building a country house. To begin with, the site must be carefully chosen where there is a good supply of wood, for building purposes and fuel, and more especially of water. For, " he the whiche wyll dwell at pleasure, and for proffyte and helth of his body, he must dwell at elbow-room, having water and woode anexed to his place or howse ; for yf he be destytuted of any of the pryncypalles, that is to say, fyrst, of water for to wasshe and to wrynge, to bake and to brewe, and dyvers other causes, specyally for peryll the whiche myghte fall by fyre, it were a dyscommodyous thynge." The position itself and the views from it must be pleasant : " I had rather not to buyld a mansyon or a howse than to buylde one without a good prospect in it, to it and from it. For yf the eye be not satysfyed the mynde cannot be contented, the herte cannot be pleased ; yf the herte and mynde be not pleased, nature doth abhorre." Next, it is very important that the air should be fresh, pure and clean ; so the neighbourhood of stagnant ponds and stinking ditches should be avoided. Inside the house care should be taken to keep the kitchen and other offices clean, so that there are only " good and odyferous savours " from them, and the rooms should not be swept until the master of the house has gone out (admirable injunction !), " for the dust doth putryfy the air, makyng it dence." It is particularly important if there is any pestilence about to keep the air sweet, by burning juniper, rosemary, bay-leaves or other aromatic herbs. And indeed such fumigation, or the use of such a pomander, or spice-ball, as Wolsey was wont to hold to his nose when he passed through the unwashen crowd, must have been desirable in old-fashioned houses ; for, forty years earlier, Erasmus had expressed his disgust at the stench of English houses, where the floors were covered with decaying rushes full of unmentionable filth. Matters improved, however, and sixty years after Erasmus another Dutch traveller in England, after praising, as Erasmus had done, the incredible courtesy and friendliness of the English, added : " And beside this, the neat cleanliness, the exquisite finenesse, the pleasaunte and delightful furniture in every poynte for household, wonderfully rejoysed me : their chambers and parlours strawed over with sweete herbes refreshed me ; their nosegayes finely entermingled with sundry sorte of fragraunte floures in their bedchambers and privy roomes, with comfortable smell cheered me up and entirelye delyghted all my sences."

The house should face, if possible, East and West, but certainly not South, as, while the " the Eest wynde is temperate, fryske and fragraunt," the south wind is most unhealthy, an idea which, I think, Boorde must have brought back with him from his sojourn in the south of France. As to its plan : the hall should have a parlour annexed to its upper end, while at the lower end should be the buttery and pantry, with a cellar under the pantry, and the kitchen, larder, etc., beyond them. The " lodgings," or bedrooms, should be placed round the court, and in the centre of the side opposite the hall should be the gatehouse. The chapel, then a necessary part of every large house, should be so arranged that the " chambre of astate," or best bedroom, and as many other chambers as possible, should look into it.

There might well be an outer court, containing the stable for riding-horses and necessary buildings, but anything in the nature of farm-buildings, including the dairy, brew house and bake house, should be well away from the house.

Although the Elizabethan builders for the most part abandoned the old arrangement round a central courtyard, the tradition was to some extent kept up in many instances by

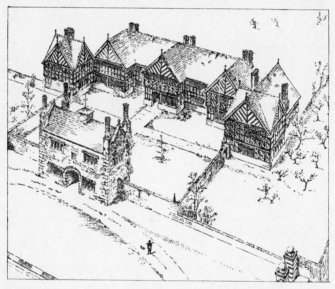

23. HOUSE WITH FORE-COURT AND GATEHOUSE

(KENYON PEEL HALL, NEAR TYLDESLEY)

the presence of a walled forecourt in front of the house, with a gate-house, or at least an entrance of some architectural pretensions (see Fig. 23). A favourite plan for the house itself was that of a central block with wings projecting at right angles from the ends, forming with a central porch the shape of an E. The central block contained the hall, which, as we have said, by this time usually served as a vestibule leading to the other parts of the house and containing the great staircase ; the wings afforded space for the living rooms and bed-chambers, which had become more numerous with

PLATE XXXVI

THE LONG GALLERY, ASTON HALL

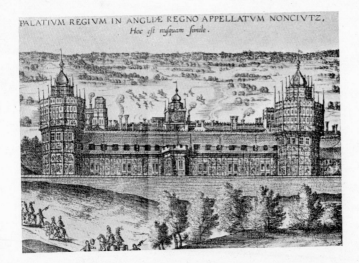

NONSUCH PALACE

PLATE XXXVII

COWDRAY, SUSSEX

HARDWICK HALL, DERBYSHIRE

24. KENYON PEEL HALL, NEAR TYLDESLEY

the increase of privacy and comfort.   At the angles formed
by the wings with the main block turrets were often built,
which, with the massive and often ornate chimney stacks,
served to break the lines of the roof.   Lightness was also
given to the design, as well as to the interior, by the number
and size of the windows, which were occasionally multiplied
to an excessive extent, notoriously at " Hardwick Hall, more
window than wall " (see Plate XXXVII).   Even in the
most exaggerated cases, however, the fact that the windows
were divided by stone mullions and transoms into small
panels and that the glass was in small leaded quarries avoided
the bare and staring effect of modern sash-windows filled
with plate-glass.   The materials of which the houses were
built naturally varied with the district.   Many of the smaller
houses were still built mainly of timber and plaster, and the
same materials were used with very picturesque effect, for
more important buildings (see Fig. 24), particularly in Lan-
cashire and Cheshire.   Where stone was abundant it was
used ; but on the whole the most typically Tudor material
was brick, and from an artistic point of view few substances
are more satisfactory to look upon than these narrow, rich,
red bricks, with their irregularities of surface and colour.

Internally the walls might be " either hanged with
tapestry, arras work or painted cloths, wherein either divers
histories, or herbs, beasts, knots and such like are stained, or
else they are ceiled with oak of our own or wainscot brought
hither out of the east countries, whereby the rooms are not
a little commended, made warm and much more close than
otherwise they would be."   On the whole it may be said
that hangings of Flemish tapestry, such as Cardinal Wolsey
loved, were more typical of the first half of the century, and
panelling in oak, often ornamented with the " linen-fold "
pattern, of the latter half.   The decoration of walls with
painted patterns or pictures was also not uncommon and at the
very end of the period wall-papers, printed from wooden
blocks, began to make their appearance.   The fire-places
tended to become the central feature of the rooms and ornament was lavished upon them (see Fig. 25) ; carved chimney
breasts and overmantels of wood or stone, painted and gilt,
served to display the heraldic pomp of the owner or the

artistic ingenuity of the craftsman, which the massively ornate iron fire-backs and dogs, or andirons, served to accentuate. Plaster ceilings came gradually into fashion, and in the greater houses were often moulded into patterns of great richness, which with their play of light and shadow

25. THE GREAT CHAMBER, SOUTH WRAXALL, WILTS

formed a most attractive feature of the rooms. On the floors the insanitary rushes gradually gave way to straw-matting and carpets, or rather rugs—a change which brought with it an improvement in cleanliness and table-manners.

Of furniture there was, even in the houses of the wealthy, astonishingly little, and that massive and simple. In the hall there would probably be three tables, that on the dais long and narrow, its legs ornamented with the carved knops characteristic of the period, while the other two would be moveable boards on trestles ; some forms, a chair and a few stools ; a dozen cushions, a hanging chandelier, a chest or two and certainly a cupboard.   On the cupboard was set out the gilt and silver plate for which English households were famous.   Noblemen had often plate worth one or two thousand pounds (says £10,000 in modern money), merchants and gentlemen five hundred pounds and upwards.

26. A TABLE

An inventory of the goods of a well-to-do citizen of London in 1488, before this form of ostentation had reached its height, shows that he had, amongst other articles of silver, six salts, two covered cups, nine goblets, twenty-seven bowls, " a Spanysshe spyce dysshe," two ginger forks, four dozen spoons, a barber's basin and a bell ; while the inventories of great lords and royal households read like descriptions of Aladdin's cave.

In the bed-rooms the chief object was, of course, the bed. The more important beds were of the four-poster type, consisting of a great shallow box, raised above the ground and supported by a post at each corner, the tops of the posts being

connected by a rail or cornice (see Fig. 27). Behind the
head of the bed was the " tester," a panel of tapestry, embroidery or carved wood ; from the cornice hung curtains,
and across the top stretched the " sperver " or ceiling, which
again might be either of stuff or of wood. Many of the
bedsteads were covered with a wealth of carved and gilded
ornament, their hangings, valance and counterpanes of rich
materials elaborately embroidered, and were worth great

27. A BEDROOM, ASTLEY HALL

sums of money. Nor were they instances of magnificent
discomfort, but on the contrary well adapted for the main
purpose of a bed—sleep. The exact procedure for the
making of the king's bed was laid down in great detail in
certain Household Ordinances of Henry VII and applied,
with the omission of ceremonious observances, to the making
of any beds of this type. First a layer of straw was put into
the box of the bedstead : it was the duty of a yeoman of the
chamber to roll up and down on this straw, not so much in
order to smooth it as to make sure that no daggers or other
treacherous weapons had been hidden in it. Over the straw

G

was placed a piece of canvas and on that a feather-bed ; when this had been well beaten and smoothed with a bed-staff a blanket was stretched over it, and then a sheet. When the sheet and blanket had been tucked in all round the feather-bed the second sheet was put on, followed by a blanket, a rug of ermine and another fur rug. The head of the bed was then turned down and the pillows, which had been well beaten, laid in place and covered with a head-sheet of linen, and on that another head-sheet of ermine, over which the linen head-sheet was turned back. Finally the whole bed was covered over with a linen sheet and the curtains drawn all round. While such was the luxurious resting-place of the wealthy, men of humbler rank naturally fared harder, though in all classes the standard of comfort was rising, for Harrison in 1577 tells us that one of the things which most struck old men to whom he had talked in the village was :—

" the great (although not general) amendment of lodging ; for, said they, our fathers, yea and we ourselves also, have lain full oft upon straw pallets, on rough mats covered only with a sheet, under coverlets made of dagswain or hopharlots (I use their own terms), and a good round log under their heads instead of a bolster or pillow. If it were so that our fathers, or the goodman of the house, had within seven years after his marriage purchased a mattress or flock bed, and thereto a sack of chaff to rest his head upon, he thought himself to be as well lodged as the lord of the town, that peradventure lay seldom in a bed of down or whole feathers, so well were they content and with such base kind of furniture ; which also is not very much amended as yet in some parts of Bedfordshire and elsewhere further off from our southern parts. Pillows (said they) were thought meet only for women in child-bed. As for servants, if they had any sheet above them it was well, for seldom had they any under their bodies to keep them from the pricking straws that ran oft through the canvas of the pallet and raised their hardened hides."

All through the Middle Ages it had been the custom for

persons of all classes to lie in bed naked, except for a night-cap, and this certainly continued to be usual throughout the Tudor Period, but by the time of Elizabeth some of the more advanced families seem to have adopted the habit of wearing night-clothes.

Beyond the bed, which it-self served as a couch when the bed-chamber was used as a reception room, there was little furniture in the chamber ; a chair, a chest or two and a press, or closed cup-board, to contain clothes, and a flat-topped cupboard to carry a basin and ewer—of baths we seem to find fewer traces in Tudor than in medieval times. The greatest display of furniture and ornaments would proba-bly be found in the long gallery, which has already been mentioned as a feature of the Elizabethan house. Here there might be a num-ber of tables and several chairs, covered with stamped and gilded Spanish leather or embroidered velvet, possibly even an invalid chair like that which Lord Talbot sent to the gouty Lord Burghley, "a clothe chayre, such an other as I devised with my upholster not long synce and sent to my Lorde my father ;

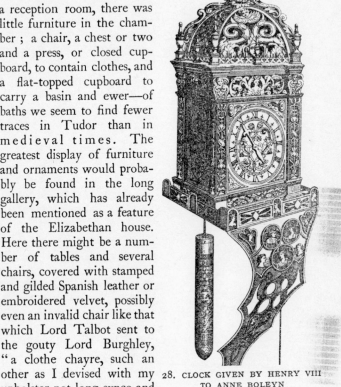

28. CLOCK GIVEN BY HENRY VIII
TO ANNE BOLEYN

when your lordship shalbe occasioned to longe in your chamber, I hope you may fynde some ease in a devise in it to lay up your leg." Here also, on the walls, besides tapestries and portraits, would very likely hang

Venetian glass mirrors or other mirrors of polished metal, and, on a bracket, a clock. Such a clock might, like some of those belonging to Henry VIII (see Fig. 28), have bells on which the hours were struck by little figures of men, or a chime, or even a " larum " ; sometimes they showed the phases of the moon or " all the days of the year and the planets," and indeed Henry had one " rounde cloke of iron with sundry dores of copper graven showing howe the sea doth ebbe and flowe, with a case of glasse sett in iron gilt, standing upon a foote of wood." In the gallery also might be musical instruments—a little organ, virginals or harpsichord, a viol, lute or case containing flutes. For here was passed the main part of the social life of the house that did not centre round the dining-table.

The English have always been noted as great eaters ; " Our English nature cannot live by roots, by water herbs, or such beggary baggage," as one who wrote in the days of Edward VI said, complaining that the great rise in the price of meat had put it out of the reach of the peasantry. On this, as on many other subjects, Dr. Boorde gave good advice : " Two meales a daye is suffycyent for a resting man ; and a labourer may eate three tymes a daye ; and he that doth eate ofter, lyveth a beestly lyfe. . . . Also sondry meates eaten at one meale is not laudable ; nor it is not good to syt long at dyner and supper. An houre is suffycyent to syt at dynner ; and not so longe at supper." Further, he points out the foolishness of beginning with heavy meats and only putting on the better, light and nutritive meats when the appetite has already been blunted, so that either the best food is left for the servants or the diner eats through greed what he does not require. Few, however, of the rich followed his precepts ; if they kept to the two or three meals, they made their dinners and suppers occasions of lavish display, particularly in Elizabeth's days. Harrison says : " In number of dishes and change of meat the nobility of England (whose cooks are for the most part musical-headed Frenchmen and strangers) do most exceed, sith there is no day in manner that passeth over their heads wherein they have not only beef, mutton, veal, lamb, kid, pork, cony, capon, pig, or so many of these as the season yieldeth, but

PLATE XXXVIII

THE HOUSEWIFE

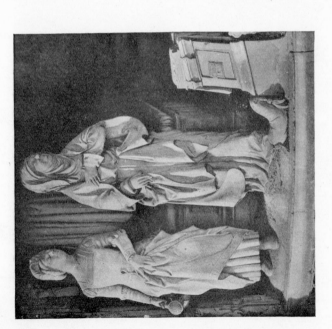

A LADY AND HER MAID

PLATE XXXIX

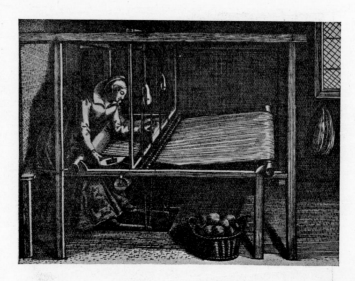

SPINNING AND WEAVING

also some portion of the red or fallow deer, beside great
variety of fish and wild fowl, and thereto sundry other
delicates where in the sweet hand of the seafaring Portugal
is not wanting." He, indeed, partly excuses the prodigality
on the ground that the great men eat little of it themselves,
but most of it goes to the guests and servants and what is
left over to the poor. But Stubbes, after deploring that
" nowadaies, if the table be not covered from the one end to
the other as thick as one dish can stand by another, and to
every dish a severall sawce appropriat to his kinde, it is
thought unworthye the name of a dinner," demolishes the
excuse of provision for the poor, declaring that they get

nothing but "the refuse
meat, scraps and par-
ings, such as a dog
would scarse eat some-
times ; and well if they
can get that too ; in-
stead whereof not a
few have whipping
cheer to feed them
withall." Another con-
temporary writer says :
" The poore with us

29. THE COOK

woulde think themselves happy if they might have a messe of
potage, or the scraps that come from the rich mens table, two
or three hours after they begin their dinner or supper, and to
have the same given them at their doore. But many of the
said rich greedie guttes, caring for nothing but for the hilling
and filling of their owne backe and bellie, can not be content
to goe by their poore pitiful brethren and give them nothing,
but they will most uncharitably and unchristianly rebuke
them, chide them, rattle them, yea, and threat them, that the
poore, being checkt of them that shoulde chearishe them,
are almost driven to despaire."

Some idea of the prodigious provision made upon exceptional occasions may be gathered from the expenditure
on food at Lord North's house when Queen Elizabeth
stayed there for three days in 1577. The bread alone
required 17½ quarters of wheat ; 67 sheep and 34 pigs were

consumed ; four stags and sixteen bucks were used to make
176 pasties ; 1,200 chickens, 363 capons, 33 geese, 6
turkies, 237 dozen pigeons and quantities of partridges,
pheasants, snipe and all kinds of other birds, including gulls ;
a cartload and two horseloads of oysters ; fish in endless
variety ; 2,500 eggs and 430 pounds of butter are among
the items.   Even to read an ordinary Elizabethan cookery
book induces a feeling of respect for those spacious days
when one could be cheerfully bidden, " take a dozen or
sixteen eggs," " take a quart of cream," or, in order to make
a simple jelly, " Take two calves feet and a shoulder of veale,
and sette it upon the fyre in a fayre potte wyth a gallon of
water and a gallon of claret wyne, then lette it boyle till it
be jellye, and then take it up and drayne it and putte thereto
synamon, ginger and suger and a lyttle turnesole to coloure
it after youre dyscrecion."

Moreover, if the food was lavish in quantity and quality
it was also served in the houses of the great with ceremony
worthy of a religious ritual.   In Viscount Mountague's
kitchen at Cowdray no one might " stande unseemely with
his backe towarde his meate while it is at the raunge," and
when it was carried through the hall to his private dining
chamber all had to uncover respectfully as it went by.   Even
the preliminary laying of the table had to be done with
obeisances and genuflexions and the Yeoman Usher was
solemnly charged to kiss the table-cloth before he placed it
upon the table.   On ordinary days the Viscount was content
that his food should be brought in by the Usher, with at
least six Gentlemen or Yeomen in attendance, but on special
occasions when he dined in the hall the procession to the
upper table was headed by his Steward and Comptroller in
fair gowns, with white staves in their hands, with the Mar-
shall and two Ushers.   But, for all that, the Viscount still
ate with his fingers and not with a fork.

Among men of less rank and wealth there was naturally
less lavish provision.   " The gentlemen and merchants
keep much about one rate, and each of them contenteth
himself with four, five or six dishes, when they have but
small resort, or peradventure with one, or two, or three at
the most, when they have no strangers to accompany them

at their tables." They were also not above having a hot joint sent in again next day cold. But when a merchant gave a feast " it is a world to see what great provision is made of all manner of delicate meats, from every quarter of the country, wherein . . . they will seldom regard anything that the butcher usually killeth, but reject the same as not worthy to come in place. In such cases also jellies of all colours, mixed with a variety in the representation of sundry flowers, herbs, trees, forms of beasts, fish, fowls and fruits, and thereunto marchpane wrought with no small curiosity, tarts of divers hues and sundry denominations, conserves of old fruits, foreign and home-bred, suckets, codinacs, marmalades, marchpane, sugar-bread, gingerbread, florentines, wild fowls, venison of all sorts, and sundry outlandish confections, altogether seasoned with sugar, do generally bear the sway." The prevailing notes of Tudor cookery were spices, pies and sugar. Meats, vegetables, fruits and flowers, such as primroses and marigolds, were made up into pies, pastries and tarts ; nine out of ten recipes contained spices ; and all kinds of meat, from crab to venison, were eaten with sweet sauces. It is of some interest to note that in 1572 in London sugar cost a shilling the pound, " kytchin suger " being 10d., ginger 4s., cloves 6s. 6d., cinnamon 4s. 6d., raisins 3½d., currants 9d., and rice 4d., all of which prices have to be multiplied by about ten to give the equivalent in modern money.

The gentry usually dined at eleven, sometimes sitting over their meal till two or three in the afternoon, and supped about six o'clock. Merchants and farmers dined at noon, and the latter did not usually sup before seven or eight. The farmer and craftsman fed on plain substantial joints, helped out with bacon, fowls, fruit, cheese, butter and eggs and flavoured with appetite and good fellowship. " Both the artificier and the husbandman are sufficiently liberal and very friendly at their tables ; and when they meet they are so merry without malice, and plain without inward Italian or French craft and subtlety, that it would do a man good to be in company among them. Herein only are the inferior sort somewhat to be blamed, that being thus assembled their talk is now and then such as savoureth of scurrility and ribaldry, a thing naturally incident to carters and clowns, who think themselves not to be merry and welcome if their foolish veins in this behalf be never so little restrained. . . . If they happen to stumble upon a piece of venison and a cup of wine or strong beer or ale they think their cheer so great, and themselves to have fared so well, as the Lord Mayor of London." On the whole, indeed, it must have been more amusing to dine with the humble than with the mighty ; for though the fare served at the tables of the great was daintier it was eaten in solemn silence and if the guests started to chatter they were liable to be rebuked by the usher saying with a loud voice, "Speak softly, my masters." True that, on the other hand, the humble were apt to become even excessively talkative—especially under the influence of home-brewed beer.

"Water is not wholesome, sole by it selfe, for an Englysshe man," said Andrew Boorde ; a sentiment with which his contemporaries thoroughly agreed. On the other hand he showed himself old-fashioned in preferring ale to beer. Beer, which resembled ale in being a fermented liquor made from malt but differed from it in being bittered with hops, had been introduced into England by the Dutch in the fifteenth century. It had already, when Boorde wrote, gone far to supplant ale in the public favour and by Elizabeth's time had almost completely ousted the older drink. Prodigious quantities of it were drunk, and every farm and house of any size brewed its own beer. Cider was also made in many parts of the country and seems to have been particularly popular in the harvest-field ; and a few persons still brewed the ancient and ambrosial mead, or metheglin—not to be confused with the "kind of swish-swash made also in Essex and divers other places, with honeycombs and water, which the homely country wives, putting some pepper and a little other spice among, call mead." Whichever the drink, it was still served in great black leather jacks, but the pottery mugs which were usual at the beginning of the Tudor period soon gave way to silver and pewter and stone-ware mugs with metal mountings, while, by the time that Shakespeare was enriching the stage with his sack-swilling Falstaff, glasses were all the fashion. In the houses of the great the glasses were of fine Venetian ware, admirably adapted to enhance the glow and sparkle of the six and fifty wines of France, which with malmsey, romney, muscadell and other wines of Italy and the Levant, were then in vogue. Humbler folk contented themselves with coarse glass of English make; but, as " golden lads and lasses must, like chimney-sweepers, come to dust," so crystal of Venice or rough Surrey glass " in fine all go one way—that is, to shards at the last, so that our great expenses in glasses (beside that they breed much strife toward such as have the charge of them) are worst of all bestowed in mine opinion, because their pieces do turn into no profit." In spite of which philosophical reflection glass continued to be used, not only for goblets, but also for candlesticks, jam jars, spice-plates and trenchers. Earthenware plates, probably Dutch ware of delft type, were just beginning to make their appearance, Henry VIII having six such trenchers in 1542, but for the most part the wealthy ate off silver or pewter and the poorer or more old-fashioned off wood, and in Elizabethan times fruit-trenchers were made of thin wood elaborately painted with verses and designs.

In no other country were such prodigious households maintained by the gentry as in England and even in the middle-class houses the number of idle servants impressed foreign visitors unfavourably. Owing their existence to the ostentation of their masters, they aped the vices and extravagances of those above them, gambling, swearing and living riotously. Even in their dress they aimed at show rather than use, wearing long coats that were nothing but a nuisance when they had to ride and doublets with such pleatings and puffings of sleeves that if they had to defend their masters or themselves they must throw off their garments before they could draw a bow. Much, of course, depended upon the strictness or laxity of the master. Such a set of rules as was drawn up by Sir John Harington in 1592 proves that in some, probably in many, country houses good discipline was maintained. His servants were to be up by six o'clock in summer or seven in winter; the hall was to be clean within an hour of their rising, and their beds made and fireplaces cleaned up by eight o'clock. When guests left, their rooms were to be tidied up within four hours ; and the stairs and other places swept and dusted every Friday afternoon. Breach of these rules, or such offences as swearing, were punished by small fines, and breakages were stopped out of wages. His contemporary, Lady Hoby, a pious and efficient lady, is shown by her diary to have kept her women servants busy, not only by precept but by example. She would seem, indeed, to have been like one of those " ancient ladies of the court," whom Harrison praises for their industry, employing their

30. CHILDREN

leisure in embroidery, spinning silk, reading the Scriptures or books of history and even writing and translating foreign works. Many of them also, he says, and Lady Hoby was among the number, were skilled— perhaps it would have been more accurate to say, venturesome—in surgery and the preparation of medicines. But a knowledge of four or five languages and of the medicinal properties of herbs did not make them less competent in household affairs, for there was " none of them but when they be at home can help supply the ordinary want of the kitchen with a number of delicate dishes of their own devising." It was, indeed, part of the training of a lady to be able to distill rosewater and other such scented and flavoured waters, and to make comfits and conserves.

In the humbler ranks of society the duties of a farmer's wife, as described by Fitzherbert in 1523, were multifarious. Rising early in the morning she would proceed to sweep the house, milk the cows, dress the children, and get breakfast for her husband, the children and the labourers. In the course of the day there would be butter and cheese to be made, corn to be measured out and sent to the mill.

NEEDLEWORK PANELS SHOWING COSTU

PLATE XL

MES OF THE ELIZABETHAN PERIOD

malt to be prepared for brewing. She would have to feed
the chickens, collect the eggs, set any hens that were broody,
and if it were market day ride off with eggs, butter, cheese,
chicken, or other farm produce. The kitchen garden
would demand her attention and she might have to lend a
hand at hay-making, winnowing corn and so forth.
Washing-day meant more hard work for her and her maids,
clothes being cleansed by violent pounding with wooden
" beetles " or clubs (see Fig. 31) and there being none of
the modern aids for the rapid removal of dirt and buttons—

though an inventory of
the Earl of Warwick's
wardrobe in the time of
Edward VI shows that
even then shirts were
lost and exchanged in
the wash. In such spare
time as she had the
housewife would ply
her distaff, spinning
wool for cloth and
blankets, or flax and
hemp for sheets, towels,
table-cloths and
smocks.

31. A LAUNDRY

So much for the in-
dustrious, but all women were not so. " For some of
them lye in bed till nine or tenne of the clocke every
mornyng ; then, beyng rouzed forthe of their dennes,
they are two or three howers in puttyng on their robes,
which being done they go to dinner, where no delicates
either of wines or meates are wanting. Then their
bodies being satisfied and their heades pretely mizzeled
with wine, they walke abroad for a time, or els confer with
their familiars—as women you know are talkative enough,
and can chat like pyes, all the world knoweth it. Thus
some spende the daie till supper tyme, and then the night,
as before." That they should take two or three hours
to dress can hardly surprise any one who has looked at
pictures of Elizabethan dames arrayed in all their glory (see

Plate XL). In a play of the period one of the characters
says : " Five hours ago I set a dozen maids to attire a boy
like a nice gentlewoman ; but there is such doing with
their looking-glasses, pinning, unpinning, unsetting, form-
ings, and conformings ; painting blue veins and cheeks ;
such stir with sticks and combs, carcanets, dressings, purls,
falls, squares, busks, bodies, scarfs, necklaces, carcanets,
rebatoes, borders, tires, fans, palisadoes, puffs, ruffs, cuffs,
muffs, pusles, fusles, partlets, frislets, bandlets, fillets, cross-
lets, pendulets, amulets, annulets, bracelets, and so many
lets, that yet she's scarce dressed to the girdle ; and now
there is such calling for fardingales, kirtles, busk-points,
shoe-ties, etc., that seven pedlars' shops—nay all Stour-
bridge fair—will scarce furnish her. A ship is sooner
rigged by far, than a gentlewoman made ready." In
dress, as in so many other things, the movement during
Tudor times was in the direction of elaboration and artificiality. The free and flowing lines of medieval costumes
gradually gave way to stiff and ungraceful formality ;
nothing but the richness of their materials and the pro-
fusion of their ornament prevents us from realizing that
the more exaggerated Elizabethan dresses were as grotesquely
ugly in design as anything produced in the basest period of
Victorian dress-making. Waists were constricted to wasp-
like dimensions with tight-lacing and whaleboned busks,
while the lower part of the dress jutted out in monstrous
hoops and farthingales. Heads were framed in exaggerated
ruffs, starched and wired, " clogged with gold, silver or
silk lace of stately price, wrought all over with needle work,
speckled and sparkled here and there with the sun, the moon,
the stars and other antiques strange to behold." From
their embroidered shoes with high heels, to their painted
faces and dyed locks, frizzled and eked out with " the curl'd-
worne tresses of dead-borrowed haire," the fashionable
ladies of the late sixteenth century were artificial. In the
Middle Ages the eccentricities of fashion had been more
noticeable in the dress of men than of women except in
the matter of head-dress. Nothing dates pictures of women
so readily as the style of hair-dressing and of head-gear.
For the first half of the Tudor century the striking feature

PLATE XLI

TIGHT LACING.

A NOBLE LADY AND HER HOUSEHOLD

PLATE XLII

ELIZABETHAN COSTUMES

A LADY OF THE MIDDLE CLASS　　　" A PALTRY CAP "

APING THE MEN

of ladies' portraits is the gable-framed head-dress that is
still worn by the Queens of playing cards. Under Elizabeth there was great variety in the materials and shapes of
hats, from the exaggeratedly high-crowned velvet hats
down to little round caps such as Katharine commended
and Petruchio denounced as " moulded on a porringer ; a
velvet dish . . . a paltry cap, a custard-coffin, a bauble, a
silken pie."

Moralists, who are apt in all ages to become slightly
fatuous when they deal with women's fashions, denounced
impartially ruffs and open-work stockings, dresses cut
immoderately low, and the even more shameful wearing
of doublets and jerkins similar to those worn by men. It
need hardly be said that their denunciations were ineffectual,
but how far they were justified is a more open question.
It is impossible to indict a nation or an age, and to say
definitely that the sex morality of the Tudors deteriorated
as the extravagance of their costumes increased might be
rash, though to deny it would be rasher still. Certainly
it is only necessary to read Shakespeare and practically any
of his contemporaries, serious or flippant, preachers or
playwrights, to realize that the standard then was low,
that seduction was considered a jest and any married woman
a fair mark for gallantries. It is true that the amiable
country parson, William Harrison, describes Elizabeth's
court as the seat of all the virtues and a model, sorely needed,
for most noble and gentlemen's houses ; but Sir John
Harington, who had spent most of his life there, sums up
life at court as " ill breeding with ill feeding, and no love
but that of the lustie god of gallantrie, Asmodeus."

A vice that was undoubtedly prevalent at the Tudor
court and in great houses was gambling. The example
was set by the sovereigns, more particularly by Henry VIII,
who is constantly found losing large sums—sixty, seventy,
even four or five hundred pounds at a time. Henry's
courtiers followed his example and Sir Anthony Fitzherbert complained of the high stakes played for : " For
nowe a poore man wyll play as great game at all maner
games as gentylmen were wont to do, or greater, and
gentilmen as lordes, and lordes as prynces, and ofte tymes

the great estates wyll call gentilmen or yomen to play with them at as great game as they do. . . . If they played smalle games, that the poore man that playeth myght bear it thoughe he loste, then myght it be called a good game, a good playe, a good sport and a pastyme. But when one shall lose upon a day, or upon a nyght, as moche money as wolde fynde him and all his house meate and drynke a month or a quarter of a yere or more, that may be well called a disporte, or a displeasure ; and ofte tymes, by the meanes therof, it causeth them to sell theyr landes, disheryte the heires, and may fortune to fall to thefte, robbery or such other, to the great hurte of themselfe and of their children and to the displeasure of God." Some sixty years later Sir John Harington said much the same at greater length, though defending the use of dice and cards to relieve the boredom of attendance at court. " Men cannot be allways discoursing, nor women always pricking in clowts " (that is to say, doing embroidery) ; it was not very amusing to listen to the prosy reminiscences of old courtiers, who " thinke that one of us may boast of the well spending of that day wherein they have told us how merry a world it was when the King went to Bullen ; whereas, thanks be to God and that noble King's most noble Dawghter, wee think it as merry still " ; and a little game of skill or hazard helped to break the monotony. But he laid down the very sound rule that " the wager in play should be as it were the sawce and not the substance of it ; so as a man should take at least equal contentment for winning the game as the money, and be less greeved for loosing the money than the game." The evil was wide-spread in all ranks of society, even the rector of Wallaton at the very beginning of Elizabeth's reign was " a common gamster at the alehouse, nyght and daye, and satt up all the nyght at the same " and on more than one occasion, having run through his money, staked and lost his horse. Efforts were constantly made to put down gambling dens and to prevent the working-class from playing games of hazard, wasting their time and risking their, and their masters', money. In fact, the laws allowed servants and craftsmen to play cards and dice only during the privileged season of Christmas.

Christmas was indeed a season of liberty and relaxation. Too much so, from the point of view of the stricter sort : " In Christmas tyme there is nothing els used but cards, dice, tables, masking, mumming, bowling and such like fooleries. And the reason is, they think they have a commission and prerogative that time to do what they lust and to folow what vanitie they will. . . Is it not Christmas ?

32. GAMBLING

must we not be merry ? Truth it is, we ought both then and at all tymes besides to be merie in the Lord, but not otherwyse ; not to swill and gull more that time than any other time, nor to lavish foorth more at that time than at another time." Rooms were decorated with holly and ivy and the household gave themselves up to feasting and jollity. Our busier and more economical age has concentrated in Christmas-day itself the rites and festivities which in those times extended to Twelfth-day, or Epiphany (January 6). Like the Scots and French, our ancestors made less of Christmas-day than of

" Newyeares day, whereon to every frende
They costly presents in do bring, and Newyeares giftes do sende.
These giftes the husband gives his wife, and father eke the childe,
And maister on his men bestowes the like, with favour milde.
And good beginning of the yeare they wishe and wishe againe,
According to the aunciect guise of heathen people vaine.
These eight dayes no man doth require his dettes of any man.
Their tables do they furnish out with all the meat they can :
With marchpaynes, tartes and custards great ; they drink with
    staring eyes,
They rowte and revell, feede and feast, as merry all as pyes."

The presents given were similar in their variety to our Christmas presents. Amongst those sent to Princess (afterwards Queen) Mary in 1544 were handkerchiefs, embroidered gloves, cushion covers, smocks, worked sleeves, brooches, books, an inkstand and sweets. On the other hand the seasonable fare does not seem to have included, as of right, turkeys, mince-pies or plum pudding. The coins and trinkets which now lurk in the pudding were then represented by the silver penny in the mighty cake made for Twelfth Night and the lucky finder was hailed as King and hoisted shoulder high to chalk crosses on the beams, as a protection against injuries " of cursed devils, sprites and bugges, of conjurings and charmes." On Twelfth Night also the boys and girls went a-wassailing, singing outside their neighbours' houses for cakes and ale and money.

During the Christmas season, in the larger houses, one of the household was appointed King of Christmas or Lord of Misrule, and under him were presented masques and mummeries. At court Henry VIII himself, in his younger days, took part in many such masques with his nobles, having an evident delight in dressing-up and disguises ; but as time went on the entertainments grew more formal and developed into theatrical displays, in which the courtiers were now too dignified to take part. A similar change no doubt took place in the country houses and the mummeries took the form of those Christmas plays— presented by Bottom the weaver, Snug the joiner and other village enthusiasts—which lingered on in some districts almost to our own times.

Though dancing and music played a large part in the

PLATE XLIII

COSTUMES IN ENGLAND

A SATIRE ON RUFFS

PLATE XLIV

MUMMERS

A DINNER-PARTY

PREPARING A FEAST

festivities of Christmas they were far from being confined to that season. Music in particular, was considered an essential part of a good education. Even if there were any truth in the Puritan criticism that music "woman-isheth the minde," it could hardly be said to be a sure sign of effeminacy, seeing that we find Henry VIII at the beginning of his reign "exercisyng hym selfe daily in shooting, singing, daunsyng, wrastelyng, casting of the barre, plaiyng at the recorders, flute, virginals, and in setting of songes, makyng of ballettes, and did set two goodly masses, every of them fyve partes, whiche were sung oftentimes in hys chapel, and afterwardes in divers other places." Henry, indeed, was very devoted to music, though such of his compositions as have survived are, according to some critics, almost as feeble as might have been expected from a royal amateur. He kept a large number of musicians in his household, and an inventory of the goods in West-minster Palace in 1542 shows a surprising number of musical instruments : there were twenty "regals," or portable organs, of varying size and make, fourteen "vir-ginals," precursors of the harpsichord, and two clavichords and something which suggests a barrel-organ, described as " oone instrument that goith with a whele withoute playeing upon, of woode vernisshed yellowe and painted blewe with six rounde plates of silver pounced with antique worke garnisshed with an edge of copper and gilt." There were also twenty-five lutes, eleven viols and seven gitterns, sixty-five flutes, nearly as many " recorders," a mild variety of clarionet, and fifteen shawlms. Scotsmen will note without surprise, remembering Flodden and Solway Moss, that to all this intolerable quantity of other wind there was but one bagpipe.

Henry's daughters were both accomplished musicians and in Elizabeth's time England led the world in music as in poetry. Byrd, Morley, Giles Farnaby, Orlando Gibbons and the madrigalists Weelkes and Wilbye are but the brightest stars in a galaxy which, after suffering tem-porary eclipse under the clouds of German influence, now shines out again in unabated brilliance. Elizabethan music continued the native tradition and remained definitely

English, taking from the spirit of the times only so much formality and artifice as sufficed to render the pattern of its tunes more rhythmical. Much of the music of our folk-songs and country dances dates from Tudor times and must have come into existence spontaneously, almost without the intervention of a composer, in those days when it came natural to men and women to express themselves in song and dance.

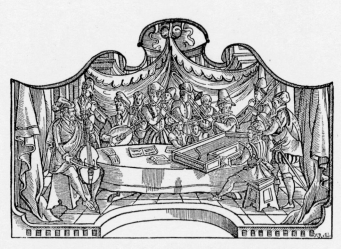

33. ORCHESTRA

PLATE XLV

Crispin de Pass inuent excudit.

MUSIC

PLATE XLVI

LUTHER, AS SEEN BY THE PAPACY

THE PAPACY, AS SEEN BY LUTHER

CHAPTER V

THE CHURCH

On no side of English life was the change during the Tudor century more obvious than in religion. But here the change was not in the direction of symmetry. On the contrary, we see at the beginning of the period a nation worshipping in forms and professing beliefs practically identical with those of their ancestors for many centuries past and with those of all the neighbouring countries of Western Europe under the supremacy of Rome. At the end of the period we see an Established Church, containing within itself a number of parties, all at variance with one another over matters of belief and ritual and only united in their enmity towards those—a large body—who still upheld the Roman form of Christianity. The Roman Church, claiming the title Catholic, or Universal, had stood in a very real historical sense for union ; the Reformed Church by the very title of Protestant usually applied to it showed that it stood for dis-union, the essence of a protest being disagreement. The Reformation, in fact, split Western Christianity into two main bodies, that of the protesters being almost inevitably, from the varying nature of the protests, bound to split up further.

In England the Reformation falls into three divisions : (1) anti-papal, approved by the great majority of the nation ; (2) anti-clerical, supported by the middle-class and many of the nobles ; (3) doctrinal (or anti-sacramental), welcomed by an energetic, and rapidly growing, minority.

The anti-papal reformation was brought to a head by the personal quarrel of Henry VIII with Pope Clement VII. The King, being unable to persuade the Pope to dissolve his marriage with Katherine of Aragon, and being equally unable to have that marriage dissolved by any one else so long as the Pope was head of the Church in England, threw off the Supremacy of Rome and declared himself Supreme Head of the Church in England and obtained his divorce from the Archbishop of Canterbury. This country had never had any great love for popes, most of whom had looked upon it merely as a source of wealth for themselves and their friends ; the papacy had recently been held by some of the greatest blackguards that even the Italian Renaissance had produced, and the papal court was a by-word for corruption and extortion ; and such abuses as the sale of " Indulgences " had offended the more thoughtful. Henry's usurpation had little obvious effect beyond diverting a certain amount of money from the foreign pockets of the Pope into the English pockets of the King. No objection to the change seems to have been felt by the laity. The clergy, who naturally cared more for the unity of Christendom and the position of the Pope as the direct successor of St. Peter, resented the change but for the most part sullenly accepted Henry's supremacy, salving their conscience by adding the formula : " so far as the laws of Christ allow." As a result, the Pope was degraded in official language to the rank of mere Bishop of Rome and declared to have no more power than any other bishop, though in actual fact he continued to rule the Church in all Western Europe except this island and parts of Germany. Among the more violent Reformers his title was usually Antichrist, or something equally impolite. The Supremacy, however, was a real fact, and the doctrine and ritual of the English Church were for the future regulated by the sovereigns or their representatives. Even the temporary restoration of papal authority in Mary's reign could only be brought about by the exercise of that supremacy which she was so anxious to renounce. Yet the final stroke in the severance of England from Rome was the bull of excommunication hurled against Elizabeth and her loyal subjects by the Pope.

The existence of much anti-clerical, and particularly anti-monastic, feeling in England before the time of the Tudors is demonstrable and natural. The clergy, as a body, possessed enormous wealth and striking privileges, which were bound to attract envy and could only be justified if their possessors maintained a high moral and intellectual standard. That a large proportion of the clergy in the fifteenth century fell deplorably below any such standard is shown by the constant complaints of their ignorance, sloth and immorality, made by bishops and other thoroughly orthodox critics, such as Thomas Gascoigne, Chancellor of the University of Oxford. If matters had amended at all during the first thirty years of Tudor rule, it can only have been to a very small degree, as Cardinal Wolsey,

34. THE SALE OF INDULGENCES

Dean Colet and Sir Thomas More are all agreed in denouncing the ignorance of the clergy and lamenting the bestowal of Holy Orders upon unfit candidates. Moreover, in 1490 the Abbey of St. Albans, one of the greatest monasteries in the realm, was found to be in a shocking state of immorality and disorder ; and Pope Innocent VIII in the same year ordered Archbishop Morton to enquire into the conditions of houses of the Cistercian and other privileged orders, where great laxity was said to prevail.

The bitter feeling against the clergy was shown in 1514 when Richard Hunne, a merchant tailor of London, who had quarrelled with his rector, was arrested for heresy and thrown into prison, where he was found hanged. Although it is probable that he had committed suicide the coroner's jury brought in a verdict of murder against the Bishop of London's Chancellor and two other persons, and the Bishop had to appeal to the King for an impartial trial, as a London jury would be certain to convict any clergyman. This bitterness against the prelates, in particular, was intensified by the greed and arrogance of Wolsey, who during the first half of the reign of Henry VIII practically ruled the realm. The fall of the Cardinal brought no popularity to the bishops ; by this time religious changes were in the air and the bench of bishops soon became divided into two camps, who supported the Old and New Religions respectively with a virulence far from edifying. Had there not been a strong anti-clerical feeling among the middle-class, whose representatives formed the House of Commons in the parliament of 1536, Henry could not have carried out his policy of suppressing the monasteries. It is true that Cromwell had, by the use of unscrupulous tools, collected such a catalogue of monastic abuses and corruption as might have shocked an assembly of inexperienced, unworldly men into demanding the dissolution of such abodes of sin. But Henry's parliaments were neither so servile nor so simple-minded as some writers have imagined. They could upon occasion amend, or even throw out, measures which the king wished passed. They were quite capable of realising that the possession of a revenue of £200 a year was not a real test of virtue, and that an Act which suppressed all houses below that figure as places of abominable living but continued all more wealthy houses (in spite of their being some of the worst offenders, according to the visitation reports) as places where true religion was maintained was not to be taken literally. We may, therefore, assert that the dissolution of the monasteries was the deliberate act, or at least had the approval, of the people through their representatives in parliament.

The fall of the monasteries had not been entirely unforeseen. In 1514, twenty years before the breach with Rome, when Bishop Foxe of Winchester founded the College of Corpus Christi at Oxford, his first intention had been to found a college for monks, but he was dissuaded by his

friend Bishop Oldham of Exeter, who said : "What, my
lord, shall we build houses and provide livelihoods for a
company of bussing monks, whose end and fall we ourselves
may live to see ?   No, no, it is more meet a great deal that
we should have care to provide for the increase of learning,
and for such as who by their learning shall do good in the
church and commonwealth."   Ten years later Cardinal
Wolsey with the assent of the Pope, suppressed about twenty
of the smallest monasteries and bestowed their estates upon

35. RUINS OF FOUNTAINS ABBEY

his new college at Oxford, which after his fall was established
by King Henry as Christchurch, and his school at Ipswich,
which was never completed.   Now the remainder of the
small houses were swept away.   Risings occurred in Lin-
colnshire and Yorkshire, of which the most formidable was
the " Pilgrimage of Grace," chiefly aimed at restoring the
monks, but the movement did not spread.   During the
next three years pressure was steadily brought to bear
upon the surviving convents and, by means of bribes and
threats, almost all the heads of the great houses were persuaded to surrender their houses " of their own free will "
to the king.   A few, notably the Abbots of Glastonbury,
Reading and Colchester, refused to be bullied or cajoled
into betraying their trust and were executed on trumped up

charges of treason. So by 1540 all the monasteries of England had passed into the king's hand.

Feeling against the parochial clergy was due to their greed and neglect of their duties. From the earliest times the duty of every man to set aside a tenth of his income for the service of God, including the support of the Church, had been recognised. The tithes—the tenth sheaf of corn, the tenth lamb or pig, the tenth of trading profits, soon became the chief endowment of the parish churches. Inevitably there was friction between those who owed and those who demanded tithes. To take a modern analogy ; it is obviously the duty of every man to contribute towards the cost of the government of his town and country, yet collectors of rates and income-tax are not popular, and where they attempt to obtain their dues by unnecessarily high-handed action there is apt to be much ill-feeling. So, when a priest, as was often the case, endeavoured to enforce payment of tithes by excommunicating defaulters, that is to say, cutting them off from the Church and so putting their immortal souls in peril, many felt that such an action was inconsistent with Christianity. Nor was it only over tithes that the clergy showed a grasping spirit. On the death of a parishioner the priest could claim as a " mortuary " one of his cattle, or, if he had no live stock, his best article of clothing or of furniture ; and in many cases the priest exercised his claim though it meant depriving the poor widow of her only cow, and practically of her means of living.

If it be urged that " the labourer is worthy of his hire " and that the clergy were within their rights, it must be pointed out that many of these clerical labourers were by no means worthy of their hire. Very often the actual holder of a church was a man, or even a mere boy, who never came near his parish. Many such men, more noble in birth than in nature, were " pluralists," holding half-a-dozen livings, and discharged their duties by appointing the cheapest vicars they could obtain. Of the resident clergy a considerable proportion were, as we have said, condemned by earnest Churchmen as ignorant and unworthy. It is not surprising that clerical writers in the early days of

the Tudors had sadly to admit the unpopularity of the
priesthood.

The parliament of 1532 struck at the crying evils of
mortuaries, pluralism and non-residence and effected certain
improvements. The coming of the Protestant Reformation
did not immediately fill the churches with a crop of angelic
ministers. On the contrary, each change—to Protestantism under Edward VI, back to Romanism under Mary
and again to Protestantism under Elizabeth—meant the

36. A SYNOD OF THE CHURCH

resignation or expulsion of the more earnest clergy, the
bulk of those who retained their livings being time-servers,
or at least men who could adapt their consciences to the
varying requirements of the authorities. There was therefore no rapid rise in the popularity of the clergy and in
London under Edward VI we find that the priests had to
be protected from the jeers, insults and even assaults of the
young townsmen. One great change in the status of the
clergy that Protestantism brought about was their right to
marry. The Roman system, by which the clergy, who
constituted possibly a twentieth of the male population, were
not allowed to have wives of their own, was open to obvious
abuses. The fact that about a fifth of the beneficed clergy

were found to be married at the time that Mary came to the throne shows that the permission was welcomed. It did, however, alter and in some ways lower the standing of the village clergyman. With men of equally high moral character (and in spite of what I have said of the corruption of the Church it must be remembered that there were always many such), the celibate priest stood more apart from the rank and file of his parishioners, unable, from his office, to

be the father of a family, he was more definitely the father of his flock. The married priest was more obviously human, and also, as he who has a wife and children has " given hostages to fortune," more dependent on the generosity of his congregation, so that the later subservience of the

37. BURNING A HERETIC

parson to the squire is largely attributable to the introduction of marriage among the clergy.

In considering the doctrinal changes of this period it is necessary to remember that England about the beginning of the fourteenth century had been greatly affected by the heretical teaching of Wycliffe and his followers, the Lollards. Although the authorities had with fire and halter suppressed the open profession of Lollardism, its doctrines still flourished in secret, and barely in secret, in many parts of the kingdom, particularly in London, and had prepared people to receive the very similar teaching of the Protestant reformers. In the opening years of the sixteenth century, before Luther had flung his challenge in the face of Rome, heresy was increasing in spite of the severity of the Church ;

so that in 1511 the King's Italian secretary, Ammonio, wrote jestingly to Erasmus that the constant burning of heretics had sent up the price of wood.   He adds that, for all that, their numbers were growing and, as an instance, even his own servant's lout of a brother had founded a sect and had actually obtained a certain number of followers. Lollard and Protestant alike rejected the supreme authority of the Church and in its stead exalted the Bible.   The Roman Church, equally acknowledging the Bible to be the message of God, claimed that that message should be interpreted to the common people by those specially ordained and prepared for that purpose, while the Protestant claimed that the message could be understood by any one "in a state of grace." It was essential, therefore, from the Protestant point of view that translations of the Bible

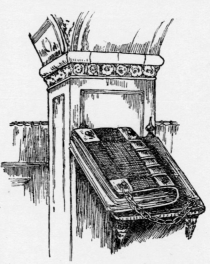

38. CHAINED BIBLE IN CUMNOR CHURCH

should be accessible to all, while the Romanists discouraged the promiscuous circulation of translations and forbade the use of any versions that had not been passed by their authorities as accurate.   When, in 1526, William Tyndale's English version of the New Testament was printed on the continent and smuggled into England, the bishops denounced it as heretical and consigned the copies to the flames, not because it was a translation but because it was a piece of propaganda, many phrases being so translated and marginal notes so worded as to attack the orthodox doctrines of the Church.   Not the least notable effect of the breach with Rome was King Henry's order, in 1538, that a copy of the

Bible in English—the " Great Bible," prepared by Rogers and Miles Coverdale, partly a translation from the Latin Vulgate and partly a revision of Tyndale's work—should be placed in every parish church for the people to study. The result was disappointing, as it led to constant quarrels and wrangling between ignorant but self-confident readers. On the other hand the Bible, in a number of slightly varying versions, became, and remained, even through the Marian reaction, a chief object of study of most Englishmen who read anything at all, and thus affected not only the opinions but also the style of the late Tudor literature.

A natural sequence to the translation of the Bible was the translation of the Church services. English prayers for private use had long been known, but in England, as in all Catholic countries, the public services were in Latin, the universal language of learning. This had the advantage that an Englishman abroad or a foreigner in England could follow the service as well as if he were in his own parish church. But it had the disadvantage that even in their own parish church very few could understand much and many could understand nothing of the service. Towards the end of the reign of Henry VIII Archbishop Cranmer compiled an English Litany, or form of prayer to be used in procession, and in 1549, after the accession of Edward VI had made Protestantism the State religion, he issued a complete English prayer-book. This First Prayer-book of Edward VI was based on the Latin prayers that had been sanctified by centuries of use and is, from the standard of pure literature, a masterpiece of English. It replaced a large variety of service-books, and in it the old services of Matins, Lauds and Prime were combined to form Morning Prayer, as Vespers and Compline were compressed into Evening Prayer. Three years later, in 1552, a Second Prayer-book, more emphatically Protestant in tone, was issued ; and this, after being abolished by Queen Mary, who restored the old Latin Services, was revived and enforced by Elizabeth, with very slight modifications (of which the change in the words of consecration which made belief in the Real Presence permissible, was the most important), and has continued in use, practically unchanged down to the present time.

The great change introduced by the English Prayer-book
was the conversion of the Mass into the Communion.   To
both parties the Eucharist was the central feature of Christian
worship.   The Roman Mass (Plate XLIX) was a service
of sacrifice, the continual repetition of Christ's voluntary
death ; the Protestant Communion (Fig. 39) was a com-
memoration of that death, suffered once and effectual for all
time.   The Catholics, holding the doctrine known as
Transubstantiation, considered that at the moment of consecration the bread and wine were converted into the actual

39. THE PROTESTANT COMMUNION

body and blood of Christ ; the Lutheran Protestants, under
whose influence the First Prayer-book was drawn up, held
that there was a mystic change by which the elements,
although remaining bread and wine, contained the spiritual
body and blood ; the Swiss school of Protestants, led by
Zwingli, held that the bread and wine were unchanged and
were merely symbolical.   From the time of the issue of the
Second Prayer-book the influence of the Swiss school pre-
dominated among the English reformers.   The doctrine of
Transubstantiation became the dividing line between the
old and the reformed churches ; over its truth men not only
disputed, but gave their lives and thought their adversaries
to have lost their souls.   For those that believed it, it was

natural to adore the Sacrament (the consecrated wafer, or Host) ; those who did not so believe, equally naturally, regarded such adoration as akin to idolatry. Each party, enthusiastically certain of the truth of their own view, regarded the other as criminally wrong-headed and sinfully obstinate.

Bound up with the adoration of the Sacrament was the whole question of the adoration of images and relics and the worship of saints—practices which had been attacked by the Lollards and were still more bitterly attacked by the Protestants. The line between religion and superstition cannot be marked, and the image which for one man may be an assistance to meditation on the merits of the saints, may for another be a talisman with magic or miraculous attributes. The Catholic Church defended the votary kneeling before an image, by saying : " He speaks not to the image that the carpenter made and the painter painted, unless he be a fool." The statement was true enough, but it made no allowance for the large percentage of fools in the population—to say nothing of the considerable proportion of knaves who were willing to exploit that folly by encouraging offerings to particular images in their own church or monastery. Possession of a miraculous image or wonder-working relics would make a church a centre of pilgrimage—local, national or European. Shrines such as those of St. Thomas (Becket) the Martyr at Canterbury and of the Blessed Virgin at Walsingham attracted pilgrims from all over Europe, some pious, some seeking cure of disease, and some merely intent on sight-seeing. Among the latter was the great scholar Erasmus, an orthodox Catholic but a man of keen insight and humour, who has left a witty account of his visit to Walsingham in about 1512, showing up the greed and ignorance of the custodians of the relics and the absurd nature of those relics. Remarkable cures did occur at these shrines, and such catalogues of miracles as have survived appear to be as genuine as the unsolicited testimonials which nowadays pour into the offices of every vendor of patent medicines ; but occasionally the merits of the pious dead were exploited for political purposes. At the very beginning of our period, when the throne of

ERASMUS

(From the collection of the Duke of Buccleuch).

THOMAS CROMWELL

CARDINAL WOLSEY

PLATE XLVIII

THE LAITY

THE CATHOLIC CHURCH

THE CLERGY

Henry VII was not yet firmly established against Yorkist rivals, the tomb of the last Lancastrian king, the godly, gentle but incompetent Henry VI at Windsor became a centre of pilgrimages ; services were compiled in his honour

40. THE SHRINE OF ST. ALBAN IN ST. ALBANS CATHEDRAL

and a plentiful crop of miracles appeared. Henry VII appealed to the Pope for the formal canonisation of his royal namesake, who was thus already informally sainted ; but the cost deterred the thrifty king and the political necessity passed away when his throne was secure. By way of contrast we may note the action of Henry VIII, after the break with Rome, in attacking the most popular of all English saints, Thomas of Canterbury. In order to discourage the clergy from resisting his authority, the King caused Becket to be declared no saint but a traitor, for his opposition to Henry II, his name to be erased from all service-books, and his bones to be burnt, a proceeding which profoundly shocked all orthodox Catholics, whose predecessors had burnt the bones of Wycliffe, as their successors, under Mary, were to burn the bones of Bucer (see Plate LI).

The degradation of Becket was accompanied by the spoliation of his shrine, which, with its blaze of jewels set in gold, was one of the most magnificent sights in Christendom. The wealth lavished upon it by twelve generations of pilgrims was now swept into the coffers of Henry VIII and its culminating glory, the great ruby given by Louis VII, of which the burning splendour is described by Italian visitors in the days of Henry VII, henceforth shone upon the hand of the King. A similar fate befell the other shrines throughout the kingdom, centres of wealth that tempted the extravagant King and of superstition that offended his conscience, grown suddenly tender—perhaps from lack of exercise. Under Edward VI and Elizabeth war was declared against images ; at first against those that had become objects of superstitious reverence, and later against all images. Statues, carved and painted altar-pieces, stained glass windows, were ruthlessly destroyed or defaced ; and the reformers were so far from St. Paul's attitude of " glorying in the Cross " that the rood, or crucifix with attendant figures of the Blessed Virgin and St. John, which in practically every church marked the division between the chancel and the nave, was torn down, and even the use of the sign of the cross in baptism was by some considered superstitious. Purgatory having been condemned by the reformers as unscriptural, prayers for the dead were forbidden and monuments with inscriptions beseeching prayers for those whom they commemorated were destroyed by zealous vandals. The walls of the churches before the Reformation were covered with paintings of scriptural, allegorical or legendary subjects ; these were now whitewashed over and replaced by neatly painted texts, perhaps more edifying for those of the congregation who could read, but certainly less decorative.

PLATE XLIX

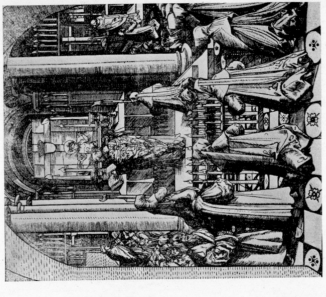

THE MASS

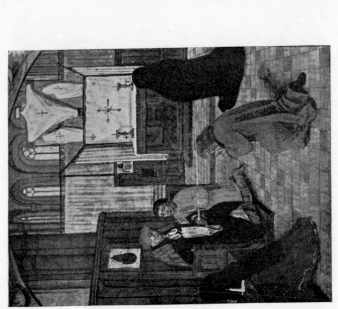

THE SACRAMENT OF PENANCE

PRE-REFORMATION SERVICES

PLATE L

LUTHER PREACHING

ARCHBISHOP CRANMER

PLATE LI

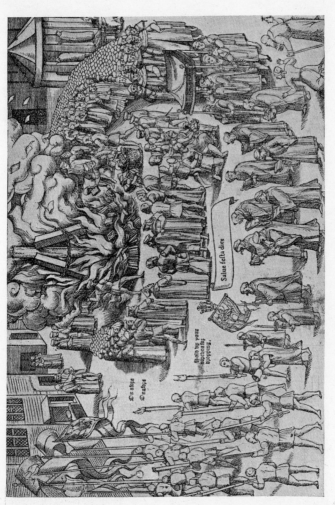

Salue fetta dies

Send bp pour
bigchtarly
hopping.

Du ddye
Prophet

BURNING THE BONES AND WORKS OF BUCER AT CAMBRIDGE

PLATE LII

WATTON CHURCH, YORK, CIRCA 1550

ST. JOHN'S CHURCH, LEEDS

41. ASTBURY CHURCH, CHESHIRE. BUILT CIRCA 1500

I

Whatever the gain in purity of doctrine, the Reformation struck a blow at the beauty of worship. The fall of the monasteries had flung into ruin many of the finest churches in the kingdom—churches not only splendid in themselves but full of magnificent monuments. Not a hand was stretched out to save these monuments of princes and great nobles. Neither their historical interest nor their beauty availed to save them. The Renaissance had brought into fashion an admiration for the art of Greek and Roman days, but for the art of the more immediate past there seems to have been little appreciation. The vast treasure of plate and jewels seized from the monasteries, including inimitable masterpieces of medieval craftsmanship, was flung into the melting pot. Later, when the commissioners of Edward VI robbed the parish churches of all but the single set of sacramental vessels necessary for the Communion, this plunder shared the same fate, a single rough list drawn up in 1550 recording the melting down of nearly a hundred thousand ounces of church plate. It is not often realised how rich were the ornaments of even the smaller churches. Many a country church possessed more plate than most cathedrals can now show, besides sets of coloured and embroidered vestments, altar frontals, banners and hangings. All this splendour was swept away by the reformers, and although the pillage was not completed at the death of Edward VI and was checked and to some extent repaired under Mary, it was resumed under Elizabeth. Moreover in the Roman service of the Mass many of the congregation did not partake of the Sacrament, and those who did received only the bread, none but the priests taking the wine ; in the reformed Communion all who were present received both bread and wine. The ancient chalices, with their small and shallow bowls were therefore unsuitable and were ordered to be replaced by " decent cups " (see Plate LIII), so that scarcely one parish in a hundred now possesses any pre-Reformation vessel.

With the less elaborate ritual came a greater formality of worship. The Catholic Church had taught that it was the duty of every man to hear Mass every day, if possible, and certainly on Sundays and Saints' days. It is fairly evident,

PLATE LIII

A COMMUNION CUP, CIRCA 1575

A CHALICE, 1527

PLATE LIV

MAP OF NORTHERN EUROPE

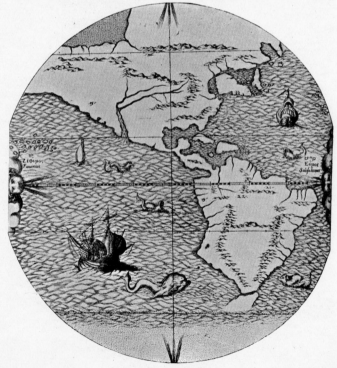

MAP OF AMERICA

however, that even those who observed this duty did not consider it necessary to be present throughout the whole service ; they came in and went out when they pleased, provided they were present at the actual moment of Consecration. Under the State Church of Elizabeth attendance at Morning Prayer was enforced by the civil authorities under penalty of a fine. By this time religion and politics had become identified ; the man who stayed away from church was evidently a Roman Catholic and it was assumed, with some justice, that he was therefore disloyal, or at best a half-hearted subject of the queen. A similar change had come about in regard to preaching. In Catholic days the priest was expected to preach and instruct his flock, but this duty was much neglected ; orthodox bishops had continually denounced the slackness of their clergy in this respect, and the

42. A FRIAR PREACHING

Protestants constantly scoffed at the Romanists as " dumb dogs." During the transitional period at the beginning of the reign of Edward VI, Hugh Latimer, himself a most industrious and spirited preacher, deplored the remissness of the bishops and clergy in preaching. On the other hand both Mary and Elizabeth had to restrain the flow of sermons, restricting the right of preaching to those who were specially licensed and confining the other clergy to the reading of " godly homilies " printed for that purpose. Regulations issued at Lincoln in 1584 are typical of the Elizabethan attitude : Mr. Jermyns was to preach on Sunday afternoons and Wednesday mornings, to teach the people their duties towards God and the Queen. One half of all the people in every house above the age of twelve, not being sick or lawfully hindered, were to be at the sermon every Sunday in the morning, and one from every house at the sermon in the afternoon of Sunday and on Wednesday ; no method for selecting the victims is laid down.   Congregations were not always appreciative and we find a parishioner of Fecken-ham getting into trouble for saying that " he would go down to the meadows and hear as good a sermon under a hedge as any made by that parson " ; while in a pamphlet made in the form of a dialogue the Capper, or typical tradesman, says to the clergyman, " In my minde, it made no great matter though we had no learned men at all . . . and as for your preaching, except yee agree better, it made no matter howe little wee had of it, for of dyversitie thereof cometh these diversities of opinions."   The truth of which is borne out by the conduct of a preacher who visited Stanford-le-Hope in 1591 and " in his sermon rayled upon the parson, calling him a dumb dog, unlerned and unstable mynister, a murderer of their sooles, with diverse other unholesome wordes and comparing him to Corah, Dathan and Abiram."   By this time, indeed, diversity of opinions within the Reformed Church had become serious and the struggle between the moderate Anglicans and the extreme Puritans had begun, which was eventually to lead to the breaking away of the dissenting or non-conformist body from the established Church of England in 1662.

CHAPTER VI

ADVENTURE ON LAND AND SEA

" To speake a word of that just commendation which our nation doe indeed deserve : it can not be denied but as in all former ages they have been men full of activity, stirrers abroad and searchers of the remote parts of the world, so in this most famous and peerlesse governement of her most excellent Majesty, her subjects, through the speciall assistance and blessing of God, in searching the most opposite corners and quarters of the world, and to speake plainly in compassing the vaste globe of the earth more than once, have excelled all the nations and people of the earth."—*Hakluyt*.

THE policy of the Tudors was on the whole peaceful, and, with the exception of the naval struggle with Spain in the last half of Elizabeth's reign, the campaigns were for the most part short and on a small scale. Yet in military history, as in so many other respects, it was an important period of transition, being the period of the development of fire-arms. Gunpowder had been used in the English armies for a century and a half before Henry VII came to the throne, but it was only under his descendants that it began to play a predominant part, and it was not until the time of Elizabeth that the hand-gun displaced the long-bow. At the very beginning of the reign of Henry VIII the growing popularity of hand-guns for sporting purposes was viewed with disfavour, the use of such weapons and of cross-bows being forbidden and the practice of archery enjoined by an Act of Parliament, which was re-enacted on subsequent occasions, but evidently unavailingly. Even as late as 1577 conservative gentlemen, such as William Harrison, deplored the decay of English archery and failed to realise that the day of the long-bow was over.

There was at this time no standing army, though Henry VII instituted a small body of permanent household troops, the Yeomen of the Guard, whose Tudor uniform is still familiar to us by the "beef-eaters" at the Tower. The cavalry, who were regarded as the most important portion of the army, were mostly volunteers, enlisted by the nobles, who were each commissioned to raise a specified number. Many nobles kept in their houses sufficient armour and weapons to equip from sixty to a hundred men ; other troopers were equipped by the towns, groups of citizens being assessed to provide their outfit. The cavalry all wore more or less complete suits of plate armour, that of the officers being elaborately fluted and often highly ornamented with embossed or engraved designs. In fact armour was never so artistically magnificent as it was at this period when it was beginning to lose much of its defensive value, owing to the penetrating power of fire-arms at close quarters. Even the infantry, or at least the picked troops, with their slashed doublets and plumed caps, their tasselled pikes and elaborate halberds (long-handled axes), were more picturesque than the troops of earlier or later days. Most of the infantry on active service were pressed men. Nominally all able-bodied men between the ages of 16 and 60 were liable for home service, and from time to time the forces of the different counties were mustered and reviewed by the Lords Lieutenants. By the musters of 1575, according to Harrison, 1,172,674 men were called up, and he reckons that probably another 400,000 escaped the summons. The same writer explains that a supply of armour was kept together in one place in every town and village, so that even the poorest village had enough for three or four soldiers, " as one archer, one gunner, one pike and a billman at the least." While the numbers of troops available were thus imposing, their quality was more calculated to strike fear into their commanders than into the enemy, as the majority were quite unskilled in the handling of their weapons. This was particularly so with the harquebuses and muskets, heavy, clumsy hand-guns which required skill and experience for their effective use (see Plate LV). At the London musters in the time of Queen Mary, most of the men being tradesmen unused to arms, " when the harquebuse was to them delivered, in discharging the same they brake their pieces, some hurt their faces and handes and some hurte their fellows and some burnte them selves with poulder, and some in giving fier caste backe their heddes, for feare the like hurte shoulde happen to them that afore chaunced to their compagnions ; whoe in so doing can give no juste levell at his enemye."

In view of the poor quality and unwieldy size of the county militia, a certain proportion were formed into "trained bands," and as there was a tendency for the wealthier members to shirk the drills, orders were given in 1599 that such defaulters should be put down for foreign service. The companies were divided into squadrons and files and began by learning the meaning of commands and of signals given by drum beats ; they then went on to marching, carrying out simple evolutions, as advancing in open order. Musketry drill began with their marching in single file past a mark and aiming at it. Those who seemed to have any notion of handling their pieces were then to be given further instruction. They were to fire first with only " priming," that is to say, the gunpowder in the pan of the musket ; having got used to the flash in the pan when the gunpowder was ignited by the match, they should fire with half charges and finally with full charge and bullet. This method would encourage many who " by reason of the churlishness of their pieces " (the harquebus probably kicked like a mule) would be frightened and " either wink or pull their heads away from the piece, whereby they take no perfect levell, but shoot at random." The degree of accuracy of fire expected may be gathered from the fact that shooting at the butts was to be at targets 4 ft. 6 in. broad at a range of 150 paces.

The picturesque chronicler, Edward Hall, has preserved for us an account of the muster of the citizens of London in 1540, when the threats of " the cancard and venemous serpent, Paule, bysshoppe of Rome," seemed likely to lead to an invasion of England. The uniform of the Londoners was white, an unserviceable colour which seems to have been popular in the army from the thirteenth to the seventeenth century. On this occasion all the wealthy citizens provided themselves with coats of white silk and adorned their basnets, or helmets, with caps of silk, plumes and golden chains, and had their halberds and poll-axes gilded. The constables had jackets of white silk, the lower ranks coats of white cloth with the arms of the City on them. The Lord Mayor, in contrast, rode in full armour with a coat of black velvet over it. His helm and axe were carried by two mounted pages in crimson velvet and cloth of gold ; and he was attended by four footmen and sixteen tall halberdiers in white silk, cut in the German fashion, " puffed and pulled out with red sarcenet," and with feathers and brooches on their caps. Besides the ordinary soldiers there were minstrels and four hundred " wyffelers," whose business was to keep the crowd in order ; and thirty standards of the city arms were borne by the tallest men of each Ward. The whole force came to the open fields at Mile End, where they " rynged and snayled," that is to say practised evolutions and formations, till all the fields seemed to be covered with a great forest of pikes. About eight o'clock they began to march ; first the field artillery, next the drums and fifes, then the captain of the gunners with four halberdiers, followed by the gunners, or harquebusiers, marching in fours, who, as they passed the King, sitting at his new gate-house at Westminster Palace, fired off their pieces. From 9 a.m. to 4 p.m. the procession, 15,000 strong, streamed past St. Paul's and the first division had gone through Westminster and St. James' Park and was back in Holborn before the last had passed St. Paul's.

Under Elizabeth troops on active service seem usually to have worn blue. Thus the soldiers sent from Liverpool to Ireland in 1567 were each to have a cassock (or sleeveless coat) of pale blue Yorkshire cloth, a buckskin jerkin and a red cap, with a yew bow, sheaf of arrows, sword and dagger ; and at the other end of the country levies from Hastings are found wearing " cassocks of blue cloth," though the colour was often left to the discretion of the local authorities. The complete outfit for a common soldier in 1599 was : a cassock of Kentish broadcloth, lined with cotton, a doublet of canvas with white linen lining, two holland shirts, a pair of " Venetians " (breeches) of broadcloth, three pair of kersey stockings, a coloured hat-cap, and three pair of leather shoes ; the officer's outfit being identical except for a felt hat and such details as silver lace and silk buttons. Unfortunately there was a great deal of fraud and dishonesty in connection with the supplying of soldiers for the army, and the authorities had constantly to complain that the men sent were " loose and ragged fellows without apparell, armour, weapon, or money in their purse," " a company of very rogues, ragged, without apparell, without armour and in such miserable case that the officers doubt the great part of them will starve for want and cold as soon as they are on the other side." Writing just after the defeat of the Armada, Anthony Marten says : " Moreover in the laying and pressing of soldiers, as there have always be great abuses in them which have been captains and had the charge thereof, so is there some corruption used at this day.   For the best and strongest bodies, the best trained and most able to do service, are many times spared, and young weaklings without strength or skill or ability are appointed in their stead."   There were plenty of Shakespeare's contemporaries who might have sat as models for his picture of Falstaff recruiting his " hundred and fifty tattered prodigals " with but a shirt and a half between them, and taking bribes to let the able-bodied Mouldy and Bull-calf stay at home.   Add to this the fact that a considerable proportion of the recruits were men let out of prison on condition of serving in the army, and it is not surprising that they deserted—in 1602 it was asserted that a quarter of the country levies ran away before they reached London—and that those who remained were undisciplined and disorderly. At Chester the troops for Ireland were continually brawling, so that it was necessary on at least three occasions to erect a gallows in the market square to overawe them.

Even on active service there was little effective discipline and the Army Regulations, though admirable on paper, were practically ignored.   Plundering might be forbidden under dire penalties, but when, as usually happened, the soldiers' wages were months in arrears, if not actually embezzled by the officers, and the commissariat inefficient, the troops were practically driven to live by robbery.   Nor was any attempt usually made to control them when a town was stormed.   There were English troops operating with the Spaniards at the capture of St. Quentin in 1553 and they appear to have shared in the orgy of murder and brutality that followed. " Frightfulness " was, always had been, and probably always will be, inseparable from war. The chronicler records with pride that in 1522 Lord Dacre and his forces on the Scottish border " did so valiantly that they burned the good towne of Kelsy and 80 villages," and English commanders record the systematic extermination of the Irish peasants with quiet satisfaction. The control of the officers over their levies was far from complete ; the army in Guienne in 1513 actually compelled their commanders to take them back to England, to the great annoyance of the King. Nor was there any reason why the troops should feel any particular devotion to their officers or to their country. Forced into the army, they suffered the hardships of war and returned to England, only too often, maimed and broken, to suffer the greater hardships of unrelieved pain and poverty. A few of the more fortunate were given places in almshouses, some obtained grants of pensions, small and grudgingly paid, and others were licensed to beg. Of the condition in which many returned a picture is given in a letter written from Rye in February of 1598 :—

" We tooke a view of the sicke and diseased soldiers in Rye and found eighty and odd that rested upon the townes charge eighte days in most miserable sorte, full of infirmities in their bodies, wonderfull sicke and weake, some wounded, some their toes and feete rotting off, some lame, the skyn and fleshe of their feete torn away with contynuall marching ; all of them without money, without apparell to cover their nakydness, all of them full of vermyn, which no doubt would have devoured them in very short tyme if we had not given them most spedy supply, whereby we were constrayned to washe their bodyes in swete waters, to take from them all their clothes and strippe them into new apparrell, both shirtes, peticootes, jerkyns, breeches and hoose, made of purpose for them."

Out of the eighty only forty-eight were saved, and many of the persons who housed or nursed them caught their diseases and died.

It was not until the very end of Elizabeth's reign, in 1601, that an Act was passed making the parishes from which the soldiers had been drawn responsible for their support ; though forty years earlier John Mountgomery had rebuked our neglect of our soldiers :—

" Suche hath been allwayes our unfriendlie and un-naturall usage and dealinge ; for at what time our warres have ended, their liveinges and wageis allso have ended, without anie further provision or other consideracion, though they were never so valliaunt and pollitique and had wone by their worthines never so muche honor to their contrie and praise to them selves. . . . Many a tall man hath lost his life upon the gallowes within thease dosen yeares ; amongest whom, as I have often heard reported, hath been manie a good souldier, who hath served in manie a sharpe shower for their princes honour. Alas ! extreame want hathe caused them to comitte such evell."

The lot of the common soldier, disbanded without pension or employment, neglected by his contemporaries, until he forced himself on their notice by turning criminal, and ignored by historians, shows the darker in contrast with the brilliant display of the noble leaders. Tournaments and feats of arms, which had been a natural feature of the fourteenth century, when fighting was the only employment of a gentleman, were revived by the Tudors and became the fashion. Henry VIII celebrated the birth of his short-lived son, Henry, in 1511 by a great tournament in which he and his noble friends took part under romantic names, the King himself taking the title, which history was to prove ironic, of " Coeur Loyal " ; on many other occa-sions, and notably at the Field of Cloth of Gold, Henry proved himself an expert jouster, and even as late as 1581 a tournament formed part of the splendid entertainment of the French ambassadors. The Tudor tournament was a sport, with umpires and an elaborate system of marking ; but, if not as dangerous as the contemporary football, it was not without risk, as is shown by the fact that Henry II of France was killed at a tourney in 1559, while Henry VIII

in 1524 was literally within an inch of receiving his death
from the Duke of Suffolk's spear. Still, it was rather an
occasion for romantic pageantry than a training for the
real business of war, in which the day of single-handed
combats was past and victory depended more and more
on the common soldiers (see Plates LVII and LVIII).

When the English army of Calais took the field in 1514,
it was in the traditional three " battailles," or divisions.
The van consisted of two wings, each of 300 men, in front
of whom went, as scouts, men from the Northumberland
borders—hardy and wary opponents of the Scots—mounted
on light horses. Then came the main division ; three
hundred German mercenaries, followed by " the standard
with the Redde Dragon (of the Tudors), next the banner
of our Lady, and next after the banner of the Trinitie,
under the same were all the kings household servauntes,
then went the banner of the armes of England, borne by
Sir Henry Guildford, under which banner was the Kyng
hymself, with dyvers other noble men and others to the
nomber of 3,000 men." On either flank of the Germans
were 600 men ; and the rearguard consisted of 800 foot
and 400 mounted lances. After them came the artillery
train, the various guns and carts amounting to 1,300, requiring the services of 1,900 men, of whom about half were
" good fightynge men." The smaller guns, such as the
falcons, sacres and minions, firing iron balls of from two to
eight pounds, up to the eighteen-pounder culverins, were
field pieces ; but there were heavy pieces, such as the
cannon and basilisk, which weighed from three to four tons
and fired shot of sixty pounds weight, and the great bombards,
or mortars, firing shot of as much as 250 pounds, which were
only employed for sieges. When a siege was to be undertaken there would also be a corps of engineers, that is to
say, miners, carpenters and smiths. For, as an officer on
the Scottish expedition of 1560 observes, " there are but
three ways of winning a fort : famine, assault and the mine,"
for which last purpose he states that " the coal-miners of
Newcastle will serve to do it." It is interesting to note
that he anticipated one of the features of the Boer War
by suggesting that some of the ships' guns should be mounted

on wheels for service in the field ; while in the Terrouenne expedition of 1514 we find a mild anticipation of " poison gas," the defensive trenches round that town containing " sundry deep pits for to have made fumigation, to the intent that men upon the assaulting of the same should have been poisoned and stopped."

It was, however, upon the sea rather than on land that England's honour and renown were most advanced—the more so that on the sea her fame rose from insignificant beginnings. Our soldiers in the past had earned undying glory at Crecy, Poitiers and Agincourt and could at best hope to recover some of their ancient, and now tarnished, fame. Our sailors had no such great traditions behind them and at the beginning of the Tudor rule were rivalled by the French as fighters and surpassed by the Venetians as traders and by the Portuguese and Spaniards as explorers. When Henry VII came to the throne the English navy had not only no history but no existence—unless half-a-dozen small merchant ships belonging to the Crown and fitted with guns when occasion required be held to deserve that title. Henry laid the foundations of the navy by building two great men-of-war, the *Regent* and the *Sovereign*, and a few smaller ships (see Plate LXI). His son took up the idea with such enthusiasm that in the first three years of his reign eight new ships were built and nine more purchased. In August of 1512 the new fleet, under the command of young Sir Edward Howard in the *Mary Rose*, encountered the French off Brest. After a preliminary cannonade the most part of the French fleet fled, but their greatest ship, the *Cordelière*, was grappled by the *Regent*. A desperate struggle ensued, but just as the *Cordelière* was on the point of capture, her magazine was fired ; the flames spread rapidly ; it was found impossible to part the two ships and both were involved in a common destruction, less than 200 of the *Regent's* crew of 700 being rescued, while of her opponent's still larger crew only six were saved. The English fleet had been capably handled and seems to have inspired a wholesome terror in the hearts of the French ; though unfortunately Admiral Howard, after blockading Brest for some time, threw away his life in a dashing but ill-advised attempt to cut out a squadron of galleys which had arrived from the Mediterranean. Galleys, propelled by oars, seem never to have played much part in the English navy. Although Elizabeth in the last year of her reign possessed six such vessels, they seem only to have been used as tugs and for ceremonial displays. Requiring crews of from one to three hundred rowers, they were very expensive, unless slave labour was available, and, although useful in the land-locked Mediterranean, were unsuitable for the open seas. In very calm weather they were formidable, and such successes as the French obtained during the reign of Henry VIII were gained with their aid. It was the galleys that burnt the little town of Brighton in 1514, and it was the galleys alone, out of all the vast fleet assembled by France in 1545, that attacked the English fleet at Portsmouth ; even then, they had to retire hastily as soon as sufficient breeze sprang up for our ships to take the offensive. It was on this occasion, as our ships stood out to sea, that the *Mary Rose* sank in Portsmouth harbour, owing to the indiscipline of the crew, who neglected to close the lee ports, so that, as she went about, the water poured in through the open ports and she went down almost in a moment, with all her crew.

The *Mary Rose*, being about 500 tons, was one of the larger ships of the fleet, of which the greatest was the *Henry Grace à Dieu*, of well over 1,000 tons, built in 1514. This great vessel carried two tiers of heavy guns, ranging from six- to sixty-pounders, while her high-built poop and forecastle each carried three more tiers of light guns. She was the pride of the fleet, and of the King, and as such was apparently too valuable to be risked in action, so that her naval career was uneventful. Henry VIII took a personal interest in shipbuilding and seems himself to have designed a type of light, quick-sailing vessel, more or less corresponding to the frigates of later days. That the Tudor shipbuilders understood their craft may be seen from the fact that many of their vessels remained in commission for fifty years or more, and that during Elizabeth's reign not a single ship of the royal navy appears to have been lost through storm or stress of weather. The growth of the navy was

PLATE LV

ARCHERY

SOLDIERS OF HENRY VIII

PLATE LVI

FIELD-GUNS, CIRCA 1600

steady ; by the death of Henry it consisted of more than
fifty vessels, of which about half were over 100 tons, six
of them being over 500 tons.   Even under Edward VI and
Mary its strength was maintained—on paper, but actually
it became very weak, a large proportion of the ships being
laid up in harbour and allowed to fall into decay, while some
of the best were hired out to merchants for trading purposes.   The result was shown in December of 1557, when
Calais was suddenly attacked by the French and was lost

43. A SEA-FIGHT

chiefly because it was impossible to get together a fleet for
its relief.   The lesson was learnt ; one of the first measures
of Elizabeth's government was to build a number of new
ships, and from the date of her accession the navy was
maintained in a state of sea-worthiness.

   The general tendency of the Elizabethan designers was
to rely more and more on the heavy guns, particularly the
18-pounder culverins, and to reduce the number of very
small guns, little more effective than mounted harquebuses,
of which early ships, such as the *Sovereign*, carried a great
quantity.   The high, many-tiered poops and forecastles
therefore tended to disappear and the prevalent type became
the flush-decked ship, without forecastle and with a low

poop, or none at all—a type far more easy to handle in stiff weather. With the change in build went a change in tactics, greater reliance being placed on gunfire as opposed to the close-quarter fighting of earlier days, when the chief idea of the combatants was to run alongside an adversary and make the fight as much as possible like a land battle. The Spaniards, with their conservative and aristocratic traditions, kept to the old-fashioned high-built type of vessel, despised the sailors as a necessary evil and manned their ships chiefly with soldiers. In the great struggle with the Armada, therefore, the main difference between the combatants was not in numbers, which were fairly even, nor in tonnage, in which the English were very little inferior, but in types. The towering Spanish ships might look to a landsman's eye more formidable than their low-built opponents, but they were far less handy and less ably handled.

Although they carried a greater number of guns, a large proportion were small pieces and they were so placed that most of their shot passed ineffectively through the sails and rigging of their adversaries, while of the heavier broadsides of the English almost every shot told on the hulls of the Spanish ships. The defeat of the Armada was important not only for its results in shattering the power, and still more the prestige, of Spain, but also as the first instance of " off-fighting " on a big scale. The Spanish captains had been ordered, before they sailed, to get to close quarters with the English, in which event their high build, their armament and the numbers of their soldiers would give them an immense advantage. The English, rather naturally, declined to come and be killed ; they hung round the Spanish fleet, pounding it from a distance, and hounded it down the Channel relentlessly. When the Armada anchored for the night off Calais, the English loosed upon them a flotilla of blazing fire-ships, before which they cut their cables and fled in confusion. When they turned to bay in the North Sea, the English resumed their pounding till the haughty Armada broke and fled, still pursued so long as the English ammunition held out under the unexampled strain upon its supplies ; after which the storms, falling

PLATE LVII

A TOURNAMENT, CIRCA 1500

A TOURNAMENT, CIRCA 1600

PLATE LVIII

CIRCA 1600

CIRCA 1500

FENCING

upon the shattered and exhausted Spaniards, completed the work of the English guns.

For the efficiency of the fleet which shattered the Armada thanks were due to such men as the renowned Sir John Hawkins, Treasurer of the Navy since 1578, and the great shipbuilding families of Pett and Baker ; but also to the patriotic enterprise of private persons. Anthony Marten, writing shortly after the victory, says :—

" Look to the amending and new building of ships ; make them strong, light and nimble for the battle. And ye that be honourable, rich and of the greatest power follow the good example of Sir Walter Raleigh, who of his own charge built two such ships the last year as, perhaps, might have saved all England in one day. Worthy of great praise also was Mr. Outrich, and Jobson of Hull, and whosoever builded the Merchant-Royal ; by the happy successes of whose ships their names shall never be forgotten."

Elizabeth herself figures chiefly in the inglorious *rôle* of an ungenerous critic of necessary expenditure and her ministers have played the usual part of Government Departments, in being blamed for not providing for circumstances more easily foreseen after the event than before. It is true that ammunition did run short ; but it had been expended on a quite unprecedented scale. The provisioning of the fleet was unsatisfactory, but certainly no worse than usual and no worse than might be expected with the primitive organisation of the period ; and if some of the beer was bad, there is no reason to believe, as the sailors did, that it was responsible for the disease which swept through the fleet. This disease, which was clearly typhus, was due to the filthy and insanitary state of the crowded ships, and was a constant peril. The great French expedition against the Isle of Wight in 1545 had been abandoned largely owing to its outbreak, and in the expedition against Spain in 1589 two-thirds of the English forces died of disease and bad food. Immediately after the defeat of the Armada we find Lord Howard writing : " the *Elizabeth*, which hath don as well as eaver anie ship did in anie service,

K

hath had a great infection in her from the beginning, soe as of the 500 men which she carried out, by the time she had bin in Plymouth three weeks or a month there were ded of them 200 and above." He adds that if the sick are set on shore, " such is the charity of the people that they shall sooner die than find pity unless they bring money with them." The disabled sailor, indeed, fared no better than, as we have seen, did the soldier in like plight ; and it must be set to the credit of Hawkins that if on the one hand he began the trade in negro slaves, so repugnant to modern ideas, on the other he founded a hospital for aged sailors at Rochester and, with Drake, established a fund for disabled sailors.

But, after all, it was neither to the ships nor to the guns nor to those that provided them, but to the spirit of those who manned them that English supremacy at sea was due. The English sailor of Tudor days believed himself superior not only to any individual foreigner but to practically any number of foreigners—and he was justified in his belief. All through the stirring annals of the time runs this note of complete self-confidence and of contempt for any English-man who would hesitate to face gigantic odds. Its climax is found in the famous last fight of Sir Richard Grenville in the *Revenge*, immortalised by Tennyson in one of the finest of all battle poems. Everyone knows how Sir Richard sooner than turn his back on the Spaniards, calmly sailed into the midst of their fleet of fifty-three ships, fought them single-handed, sinking four of them and repelling attack after attack until his ammunition was all spent, his pikes broken, half his crew dead and himself mortally wounded, when he would have blown up the ship had not the crew reasonably insisted that they might with honour save their lives by surrender. Everyone does not realise that the shattered *Revenge* was one of the only two ships of the English navy captured by the Spaniards during the whole of Elizabeth's reign—the other being the *Jesus of Lubeck*, treacherously attacked by the Spaniards at S. Juan de Ulloa in 1568, and only taken after a desperate defence. The story of the *Revenge* can be paralleled nearly seventy years earlier, in 1524, when the *Kateryne*, of 40 tons, commanded by John Mariner, with part of her crew on shore through sickness, was met off the Kentish coast by " six fayre shippes of Fraunce." The English beat off their assailants " with arrowes pykes and fightyng, and styll this continued from 4 of the clock in the mornyng tyll 9 of the clock . . . . by that tyme she had spent her pouder and arrowes with shotyng, and her bylles with hewyng, and her pykes with kepyng them off from comyng aborde, and all the company almost sore hurte, and the capitaine wounded to the death." At this point Captain Markham with " the barke of *Sandwyche* " came to the rescue. The six ships turned upon him and at last the French " with a great gunne bet downe the toppe of the barke and slewe the menne in the same, and lastly they strake doune his mast," after four hours' fighting. Even so, as long as his arrows held out the French could not board, but when they gave out they " came aborde all at ones " ; and so the two ships were taken, the English having lost 23 men and the French 27 killed and 80 sore wounded, of whom many died afterwards.

It was the same spirit that led Sir Francis Drake to " singe the King of Spain's beard " in 1587 by sailing into Cadiz and destroying 10,000 tons of shipping. In the course of this action the English encountered a number of the much vaunted galleys and came to the conclusion that four ships of the line would be a match for any twenty galleys ; while, on the way back, they captured the *Saint Philip*, a Portuguese carrack (the largest type of armed merchantman, employed in trade to the East and corresponding to the East-Indiamen of later times). " This was the first carak that was ever taken comming foorth of the East Indies," and its capture taught the English " that Caracks were no such bugs but that they might be taken "—as indeed was shown in 1592 when we took the *Madre de Dios*, of 1,600 tons, the largest ship then afloat. Nor were the men of the merchant service at all behind their brothers of the navy. In 1591 the *Centurion* of London " a very talle shippe of burden, yet but weakely manned," having in fact a crew of only 48 men and boys, successfully resisted the attack of five Spanish galleys for five and a half hours, repelling all their attempts to board her. The previous year the *Centurion* had borne her part in a battle of ten English merchant ships against twelve Spanish galleys, which had ended in the complete discomfiture of the galleys. A few years earlier, in 1586, " five tall and stoute shippes, appertaining to London and intending onely a merchants voyage " —of which the *Merchant Royal*, commanded by Edward Wilkinson, was the chief—returning from the Levant were warned that fleets of 20 or 30 galleys were lying in wait for them. " But it was neither the report of the attendance of these armies . . . . nor anything else that could daunt or dismay the courages of our men, who grounding themselves upon the goodnesse of their cause and the promise of God, to bee delivered from such as without reason sought their destruction, carried resolute mindes, notwithstanding all impediments to adventure through the Seas and to finish their Navigation, maugre the beards of the Spanish souldiers." They fell in with eleven galleys and after five hours' fighting drove them off, three of them in sinking condition, " with the losse onely of two men slaine amongst them all and another hurt in his arme, whom Mr. Wilkinson with his good words and friendly promises did so comfort that he nothing esteemed the smart of his wound in respect of the honour of the victory and the shamefull repulse of the enemy."

Tudor merchants had need of stout hearts and stout ships. Apart from the regular forces of their enemies, the seas swarmed with pirates of all nationalities. Often they were nominally privateers, licensed to attack the ships of powers with whom their own nation was at war, but they did not discriminate. In 1511, when Scotland and England were at peace, the famous Scottish rover, Andrew Barton, sent out against the Portuguese, whose ships were probably not numerous in the North Sea, " so stopped the kynges stremes that no merchaunts almost could passe, and when he tooke thenglishmenes goodes he sayd they were Portyngales goodes, and thus he haunted and robbed at every havens mouthe." At last Lord Admiral Howard " overtooke him and there was a sore battaill, thenglishmen wer fierce and the Scottes defended them manfully, and ever

Andrewe blewe his whistell to encorage his men, yet for al that, the Lord Howard and his men by cleane strength entred the mayne deck : then the Englishmen entred on all sides and the Scottes foughte sore on the hatches, but in conclusion Andrewe was taken, whiche was so sore wounded that he died there "—at which the Scottish king was most unreasonably indignant. It must be admitted that the English did their share, and more than their share, of piracy, and not without the connivance of the authorities. One of the accusations in the Bill of Attainder by which the Lord Admiral Seymour (brother of the Protector Somerset) was condemned to death was that he had encouraged pirates and shared in their plunder. During Elizabeth's reign piracy attained almost the dignity of a recognised profession. In 1563 there were 400 known pirates, many of them men

44. A SHIPWRECK

of good family ; and ten years later, when the Earl of Worcester, going on an embassy, was robbed, it is said that 900 pirates were arrested, though only three, who had been concerned in the actual robbery, were executed. All the famous seamen, with Drake at their head, who preyed upon the Spanish treasure-ships were naturally regarded by the Spaniards as pirates and can hardly be given any other title ; but that did not deter Queen Elizabeth from taking her share of their booty.

At the accession of Henry VII English trade was not very extensive ; the two most important branches were, the export of wool to the continent, which was in the hands of the Merchants of the Staple with their centre at Calais, and the cloth trade with Flanders, carried on by the Merchant Adventurers, whose continental centre was Antwerp. There was also a certain amount of trading to Gascony and Spain for wine and to Iceland for fish. A large part of the carrying was done by the ships of the Hanseatic League, a federation of the Baltic and North German ports which had risen to great power and wealth a century earlier. The merchants of the Hanse, whose English centre was at the Steelyard in London, had long possessed privileges which enabled them to trade in this country on exceptionally favourable terms, paying lower export and import dues than any other foreigners, and even than English merchants. The process of clipping their wings, which ended in the total abolition of their privileges in the last year of Edward VI, began under Henry VII, who passed Navigation Laws imposing extra duties on goods not carried in English ships. Henry VIII passed similar laws and stimulated the growth of the merchant navy by paying a bounty of 5s. a ton on all ships of over 100 tons burden built in this country. So also, under the encouragement of the two Henries, English ships entered the Mediterranean and began to bring back from the Levant those spices, silks and other luxuries for which England had hitherto been dependent upon the galleys of Venice. With the rise of the Turkish naval power, it is true, this Mediterranean trade disappeared for the first twenty years of Elizabeth's reign ; but it then revived, as is shown by the foundation of the Turkey Company in 1581.

Meanwhile the geographical centre of commerce had shifted—to the advantage of England—from the Mediterranean to the Atlantic. Throughout the Middle Ages the Mediterranean had been the channel by which the caravan-borne products of the fabled East had been distributed to Europe. The capture of Constantinople by the Turks in 1453 had closed the Black Sea route and endangered all the eastern trade. Men began to scheme how to deal direct with the spice islands of the Indies. Some considered that it should be possible to reach them by sailing westwards round the world. Of this number was Christopher Columbus, of Genoa ; but at first he could find no royal patron to supply him with ships and men. Henry VII was interested, but at the moment—in 1487—had his hands too full with establishing his own position on the throne ; the opportunity passed, and it was Isabella of Castile and her husband Ferdinand who equipped the expedition with which Columbus in 1492 discovered America, or rather the West Indies.   Five years later Henry sent five ships of Bristol, under John Cabot, a Venetian, across the Atlantic to look for the island of Cipango (Japan).   Cabot discovered an island—either Newfoundland or Cape Breton—and coasted up the mainland, which he believed to be Asia.   A second visit, next year, proved that the land was neither Asia nor a country rich in spices, and attempts made by John's son, Sebastian Cabot, and later adventurers to reach Asia by sailing round the north of America were unsuccessful and in several cases disastrous.   Disappointed in their search for a North-

45. A MERCHANT-SHIP

West passage, the English in 1553 attempted to find a North-East passage, by sailing round the north of Europe.   Although the leader of the expedition, Sir Hugh Willoughby, was lost with two of the ships, the third ship, commanded by Richard Chancellor, reached the White Sea.   From there Chancellor was taken to Moscow, where he was well received by the Czar Ivan the Terrible, with the result that the Russia, or Muscovy, Company was formed and important trade relations grew up between England and Russia.

In 1498 Vasco di Gama, the Portuguese explorer, had discovered the route to India round the Cape of Good Hope. Of this route the Portuguese kept jealously the monopoly and it does not seem to have been used by any English ship till late in Elizabeth's reign, but in 1553, a few months after Willoughby had started for the North, Thomas Wyndham sailed as far down the west coast of Africa as Guinea and the Gold Coast, even pushing inland to Benin, and from that time onwards the English traded in that district without regard to the protests and feeble resistance of the Portuguese. From the African coast also John Hawkins obtained the negro slaves with which he carried on an illegal but profitable trade with the Spanish colonies in the New World. From trading with the colonists, in defiance of Spanish prohibitions, the English soon passed to the still more profitable employment of plundering Spanish treasure-ships, their exploit culminating in the famous expedition of Drake, when, in the *Golden Hind*, of 120 tons, he passed through the Straits of Magellan and up the Pacific coast of South America, audaciously robbing towns and galleons as he passed, as far as California, and so returned by way of Java and the Cape with an astounding booty of plate and jewels.

Wonderful as are the stories of the courage and resourcefulness shown by the Tudor adventurers for trade or plunder, as set forth by their contemporary, Richard Hakluyt, in his *Principal Navigations of the English Nation*, one of the most fascinating books in the English language, in some ways even more interest attaches to the history of the first attempts at colonisation, the seed from which has sprung the British Empire. As early as 1501 a scheme was put forward for colonising the lands newly discovered by the Cabots, but, if any attempt was made to carry it out, it was certainly a failure and it was not until 1584 that any serious effort was made at colonisation. In that year Sir Walter Raleigh was licensed by Elizabeth to occupy and settle that part of the coast of America to which he had given, in her honour, the name of Virginia. It is true that the enterprise was not immediately successful and that no permanent colony was established there until a few years after the Tudor period had ended. This failure Ralph Lane, first governor of Virginia, attributed to the fact that the would-be settlers were men of a wrong type ; some had come out intent only on finding gold and silver and, being disappointed of that hope, took no further interest in the scheme ; others " had little under-

PLATE LIX

A SIEGE

A BATTERY IN ACTION, CIRCA 1600

PLATE LX

AN ARMY ON THE MARCH

PLATE LXI

SHIPS OF THE 15TH CENTURY

AN EARLY 16TH CENTURY GUN-BOAT

SHIPS OF THE TIME OF HENRY VIII

PLATE LXII

A 16TH CENTURY MAP OF SOUTH AMERICA

standing, lesse discretion, and more tongue than was needful
or requisite." "Some also were of a nice bringing up, only
in cities or townes, or such as never (as I may say) had seene
the world before. Because there were not to be found any
English cities, nor such faire houses, nor at their owne wish
any of their own accustomed dainty food, nor any soft beds
of downe or feathers, the countrey was to them miserable, and
their reports thereof according." To remedy this ignor-

46. INDIANS SMOKING TOBACCO

ance, Lane gave an account of the country, the " merchant-
able commodities " and the various food-stuffs and other
useful products, among which :—

"There is an herbe which is sowed apart by it selfe, and
is called by the inhabitants Uppowoc . . . the Spanyards
generally call it Tabacco. The leaves thereof being dried
and brought into pouder, they use to take the fume or smoake
thereof by sucking it thorow pipes made of clay, into their
stomacke and head ; whereby their bodies are notably preserved in health and know not many grievous diseases, where-

withall we in England are often times afflicted. . . . We our selves, during the time we were there, used to sucke it after their maner, as also since our returne, and have found many rare and woonderfull experiments of the vertues thereof : of which the relation would require a volume by it selfe " (see Fig. 46).

The whole account of the fertility of the country, the nature of its inhabitants, and its wonderful possibilities as a trading centre were set forth so clearly that colonists might have been expected to flock to such a Land of Promise, and it is difficult to understand—in the words of another enthusiast for the cause :—

" the fault and foolish slouth in many of our nation, chusing rather to live indirectly, and very miserably to live and die within this realme (of England) pestered with inhabitants, than to adventure as becommeth men, to obtaine an habitation in those remote lands, in which Nature very prodigally doth minister unto mens endevours and for art to worke upon."

PLATE LXIII

LANDING OF DRAKE IN VIRGINIA

EXPLORERS IN AN INDIAN VILLAGE

INDEX